A Poetry
Handbook

A Poetry Handbook

MARY OLIVER

HarperCollins*Publishers*

ecco

An Imprint of HarperCollins Publishers, registered
in the United States of America and/or other jurisdictions.

www.harpercollins.com

Library of Congress Cataloging-in-Publication Data
Oliver, Mary, 1935–
A poetry handbook/Mary Oliver. — 1st ed.
p.   cm.
"A Harvest original."
Includes index.
ISBN 978-0-15-672400-5
1. English language—Versification—Handbooks, manuals, etc.
2. American poetry—History and criticism—Handbooks, manuals, etc.
3. English poetry—History and criticism—Handbooks, manuals, etc.
4. Poetry—Authorship—Handbooks, manuals, etc.   I. Title.
PE1505.035   1994
808.1—dc20   94-49676

Designed by Lydia D'moch
Printed in the United States of America

24 25 26 27 28 LBC 56 55 54 53 52

Permissions acknowledgements begin on page 123
and constitute a continuation of the copyright page.

My thanks to Molly Malone Cook, whose unfailing support and wise counsel have, as always, encouraged and improved my work.

—Mary Oliver

Contents

The temple bell stops—
but the sound keeps coming
out of the flowers.

Bashō (1644–94)
(translated by Robert Bly)

Introduction

EVERYONE KNOWS THAT POETS are born and not made in school. This is true also of painters, sculptors, and musicians. Something that is essential can't be taught; it can only be given, or earned, or formulated in a manner too mysterious to be picked apart and re-designed for the next person.

Still, painters, sculptors, and musicians require a lively acquaintance with the history of their particular field and with past as well as current theories and tech-niques. And the same is true of poets. Whatever can't be taught, there is a great deal that can, and must, be learned.

This book is about the things that can be learned. It is about matters of craft, primarily. It is about the part of the poem that is a written document, as opposed to a mystical document, which of course the poem is also.

————

It has always seemed to me curious that the instruction of poetry has followed a path different from the courses of study intended to develop talent in the field of music or the visual arts, where a step-by-step learning process is usual, and accepted as necessary. In an art class, for example, every student may be told to make a drawing of a live model, or a vase of flowers, or three potatoes for that matter. Afterward, the instructor may examine and talk about the various efforts. Everyone in the class recognizes that the intention is not to accomplish a bona fide act of creation, but is an example of what must necessarily come first—exercise.

Is anyone worried that creativity may be stifled as a result of such exercise? Not at all. There is, rather, a certainty that dialogue between instructor and student will shed light on any number of questions about technique, and give knowledge (power) that will open the doors of process. It is craft, after all, that carries an individual's ideas to the far edge of familiar territory.

The student who wishes to write a poem, however, is nicely encouraged to go ahead and do so, and, having written it, is furthermore likely to be encouraged to do another along the same lines. Quickly, then, the student falls into a *manner* of writing, which is not a style but only a chance thing, vaguely felt and not understood, or even, probably, intended. Continuing in this way, the writer never explores or tries out other options. After four or five poems, he or she is already in a rut, having developed a way of writing without ever having the organized opportunity to investigate and try other styles and techniques. Soon enough, when the writer's material requires a change of tone, or some complex and precise maneuver, the writer has no idea how to proceed, the poem fails, and the writer is frustrated.

Perhaps sometime you will have an idea for a piece of music, you may actually "hear" it in the privacy of your mind—and you will realize how impossible it would be to write it down, lacking, as most of us do, the particular and specialized knowledge of musical notation. Why should our expectation about a poem be any different? It too is specialized, and particular.

Poems must, of course, be written in emotional freedom. Moreover, poems are not language but the content of the language. And yet, how can the content be separated from the poem's fluid and breathing body? A poem that is composed without the sweet and correct formalities of language, which are what sets it apart from the dailiness of ordinary writing, is doomed. It will not fly. It will be raucous and sloppy—the work of an amateur.

This is why, when I teach a poetry workshop, I remove for a while the responsibility of writing poems, and order up exercises dealing with craft. Since every class is different, the assignments, of course, differ too. Any instructor who agrees with the idea can easily think of suitable and helpful exercises. So can the students themselves.

When each workshop member is at the same time dealing with the same technique, and is focusing as well on the same assigned subject matter, these exercises also are of great help in making any gathering of writers into an attentive and interacting class. Each writer quickly becomes interested in, and learns from, the work of the other members.

A poet's interest in craft never fades, of course. This book is not meant to be more than a beginning—but it is meant to be a good beginning. Many instructors, for whatever reasons, feel that their "professional" criticism (i.e., opinion) of a student's work is what is called for. This book is written in cheerful disagreement with that feeling. It is written in an effort to give the student a variety of technical skills—that is, options. It is written to empower the beginning writer who stands between two marvelous and complex things—an experience (or an idea or a feeling), and the urge to tell about it in the best possible conjunction of words.

As a room may be lighted by only a few dazzling paintings of the world's many, so these pages are illuminated by a handful of wonderful poems. It is a gesture only. There is no way to include half of what I would like to include—not enough money to pay for them, not enough paper to print them! Anyone who uses this handbook is expected to be reading poems also, intensely and repeatedly, from anthologies. Or, even better, from the authors' own volumes.

A Poetry Handbook was written with writers of poetry most vividly in my mind; their needs and problems and increase have most directly been my concerns. But I am hopeful that readers of poetry will feel welcome here, too, and will gain from these chapters an insight into the thoughtful machinery of the poem, as well as some possibly useful ideas about its history, and, if you please, some idea also of the long work and intense effort that goes into the making of a poem. The final three chapters are especially directed toward issues important to the writer of poems, but here too the reader of poems is heartily welcome.

Throughout the book I have used the following phrases interchangeably: the student, the beginning writer, the writer.

Getting Ready

IF ROMEO AND JULIET had made appointments to meet, in the moonlight-swept orchard, in all the peril and sweetness of conspiracy, and then more often than not failed to meet—one or the other lagging, or afraid, or busy elsewhere—there would have been no romance, no passion, none of the drama for which we remember and celebrate them. Writing a poem is not so different—it is a kind of possible love affair between something like the heart (that courageous but also shy factory of emotion) and the learned skills of the conscious mind. They make appointments with each other, and keep them, and something begins to happen. Or, they make appointments with each other but are casual and often fail to keep them: count on it, nothing happens.

The part of the psyche that works in concert with consciousness and supplies a necessary part of the poem—the heat of a star as opposed to the shape of a star, let us say—exists in a mysterious, unmapped zone:

not unconscious, not subconscious, but *cautious*. It learns quickly what sort of courtship it is going to be. Say you promise to be at your desk in the evenings, from seven to nine. It waits, it watches. If you are reliably there, it begins to show itself—soon it begins to arrive when you do. But if you are only there sometimes and are frequently late or inattentive, it will appear fleetingly, or it will not appear at all.

Why should it? It can wait. It can stay silent a lifetime. Who knows anyway what it is, that wild, silky part of ourselves without which no poem can live? But we do know this: if it is going to enter into a passionate relationship and speak what is in its own portion of your mind, the other responsible and purposeful part of you had better be a Romeo. It doesn't matter if risk is somewhere close by—risk is always hovering somewhere. But it won't involve itself with anything less than a perfect seriousness.

For the would-be writer of poems, this is the first and most essential thing to understand. It comes before everything, even technique.

Various ambitions—to complete the poem, to see it in print, to enjoy the gratification of someone's comment about it—serve in some measure as incentives to the writer's work. Though each of these is reasonable, each is a threat to that other ambition of the poet, which is to write as well as Keats, or Yeats, or Williams—or whoever it was who scribbled onto a page a few lines whose force the reader once felt and has never forgotten. Every poet's ambition should be to write as well. Anything else is only a flirtation.

And, never before have there been so many opportunities to be a poet publicly and quickly, thus achieving the easier goals. Magazines are everywhere, and there are literally hundreds of poetry workshops. There is, as never before, company for those who like to talk about and write poems.

None of this is bad. But very little of it can do more than start you on your way to the real, unimaginably difficult goal of writing *memorably*. *That* work is done slowly and in solitude, and it is as improbable as carrying water in a sieve.

A final observation. Poetry is a river; many voices travel in it; poem after poem moves along in the exciting crests and falls of the river waves. None is timeless; each arrives in an historical context; almost everything, in the end, passes. But the desire to make a poem, and the world's willingness to receive it—indeed the world's need of it—these never pass.

If it is *all* poetry, and not just one's own accomplishment, that carries one from this green and mortal world—that lifts the latch and gives a glimpse into a greater paradise—then perhaps one has the sensibility: a gratitude apart from authorship, a fervor and desire beyond the margins of the self.

Reading Poems

MANY OF MY STUDENTS would spend almost all of their time writing and very little of it reading the poems of other poets, if they and not I were setting the assignments. Sometimes I don't blame them. There are so many poets!

But, to write well it is entirely necessary to read widely and deeply. Good poems are the best teachers. Perhaps they are the only teachers. I would go so far as to say that, if one must make a choice between reading or taking part in a workshop, one should read.

Of course, looking through books of poems to find one's particular instructors and mentors takes considerable time. Here are two things you might remember when you go into a bookstore or library and begin looking into the hundreds of books.

Time—a few centuries here or there—means very little in the world of poems. The Latin poets, the Vic-

torian poets, the Black Mountain poets—they all left us
poems that are of abiding interest. The subjects that stir
the heart are not so many, after all, and they do not
change. Styles change, and the historical backgrounds
change, but these are only peripheral matters.

In looking for poems and poets, don't dwell on the
boundaries of style, or time, or even of countries and
cultures. Think of yourself rather as one member of a
single, recognizable tribe. Expect to understand poems
of other eras and other cultures. Expect to feel intimate
with the distant voice. The differences you will find
between *then* and *now* are interesting. They are not
profound.

Remember also that there is more poetry being writ-
ten and published these days than anyone could possibly
keep up with. Students who consider it necessary to
keep abreast of current publications will never have time
to become acquainted with the voices of the past. Believe
me, and don't try. Or, at least, don't give up the time
that you need to get acquainted with Christopher Smart,
or Li Po, or Machado.

But perhaps you would argue that, since you want
to be a *contemporary* poet, you do not want to be too
much under the influence of what is old, attaching to
the term the idea that old is old hat—out-of-date. You
imagine you should surround yourself with the modern
only. It is an error. The truly contemporary creative force
is something that is built out of the past, but with a
difference.

Most of what calls itself contemporary is built,
whether it knows it or not, out of a desire to be *liked*.

It is created in imitation of what already exists and is already admired. There is, in other words, nothing new about it. To be contemporary is to rise through the stack of the past, like the fire through the mountain. Only a heat so deeply and intelligently born can carry a new idea into the air.

Imitation

YOU WOULD LEARN very little in this world if you were not allowed to imitate. And to repeat your imitations until some solid grounding in the skill was achieved and the slight but wonderful difference—that made you *you* and no one else—could assert itself. Every child is encouraged to imitate. But in the world of writing it is originality that is sought out, and praised, while imitation is the sin of sins.

Too bad. I think if imitation were encouraged much would be learned well that is now learned partially and haphazardly. Before we can be poets, we must practice; imitation is a very good way of investigating the real thing.

The profits are many, the perils few. A student may find it difficult to drop an imitated style if that style is followed intensely and for a long period. This is not likely to happen, however, when a writer moves from one style or voice to another.

When we have learned how to do something well, in the world generally, we say it has become "second nature" to us. Many are the second natures that have taken up residence inside us, from the way Aunt Sally threads a needle to the way Uncle Elmer votes. It demands, finally, a thrust of our own imagination—a force, a new idea—to make sure that we do not *merely* copy, but inherit, and proceed from what we have learned. A poet develops his or her own style slowly, over a long period of working and thinking—thinking about other styles, among other things. Imitation fades as a poet's own style—that is, the poet's own determined goals set out in the technical apparatus that will best achieve those goals—begins to be embraced.

Poetry of the Past

The poems of the past, however, present a singular and sometimes insurmountable problem. You can guess what it is: metrics.

Poems written with rhyme and in a fairly strict metrical pattern, which feel strange and even "unnatural" to us, were not so strange to our grandparents. They heard such poems in their childhood—poems by Whittier, Poe, Kipling, Longfellow, Tennyson—poems by that bard of the nursery, Mother Goose. In their literary efforts, imitating what they had heard, they wrote poems in meter and rhyme. It came, you might say, naturally.

On the other hand, we who did not enjoy such early experiences with meter and rhyme have to study prosody as though it were a foreign language. It does not come to us naturally. We too write our early poems in imitation of the first poems we heard. More often than not, they have a flush left margin, and an image or two. They do not have a metrical design.

Acquaintance with the main body of English poetry is absolutely essential—it is clearly the whole cake, while what has been written in the last hundred years or so, without meter, is no more than an icing. And, indeed, I do not really mean an acquaintanceship—I mean an engrossed and able affinity with metrical verse. To be without this felt sensitivity to a poem as a *structure of lines and rhythmic energy and repetitive sound** is to be forever less equipped, less deft than the poet who dreams of making a new thing can afford to be. Free verse, after all, developed from metrical verse. And they are not so very different. One is strictly patterned; one is not. But both employ choice of line-length, occasional enjambment, heavy and light stresses, etc.

Of course I don't suggest a return to metrical verse. Neither do I mean to suggest that the contemporary poem is any less difficult or complex than poems of the past. Nor am I advocating, necessarily, that students begin the remedy by writing metrical verse. I would like to. But it would be a defeating way to begin. The affinity is that strong with what we grow up with, the lack of affinity that powerful with what we do not. Now and again a fortunate student may discover an aptitude for

---

*Such a lack of affinity should worry English departments as well as creative writing departments, I think. How much of the poem's effect is missed by students who are not really familiar with metrics and the other devices of construction? The poem is always a blending of statement and form, which is intentional and meant to be clarifying. But this is not generally reckoned with.

metrical verse. But most students will simply struggle beyond the fair return of their time and effort.

Conventionally, English and American literature are studied chronologically—according to historical passage—and without doubt this is the best way, as central motivations and ideas, moving from one to another, should be thought about in consecutive order. But this chronology is not so necessary for the creative writing student—and, in fact, the presentation of metrical verse *first* is often so off-putting that it is worthwhile letting it rest on the tracks. There is much to be said for the idea of reading, talking about, and imitating contemporary—and I mean *congenial* contemporary—poems first, and then, later, as students become more confident, ambitious, and sophisticated, suggesting that they move on to (or back to) the difficult patterns of metrical verse.

Every poem contains within itself an essential difference from ordinary language, no matter how similar to conversational language it may seem at first to be. Call it formality, compression, originality, imagination—whatever it is, it is essential, and it is enough for students to think about without, in addition, tending to metrics. One wants the student to understand, and hopefully soon, that the space between daily language and literature is neither terribly deep nor wide, but it does contain a vital difference—of intent and intensity. In order to keep one's eyes on this central and abiding difference, the student must not get lost, either in structure or statement, but must be able to manage both. And language, as one naturally knows language, is the medium that will be quick and living—the serviceable clay of one's thoughts. And *not* what is, essentially, a new language.

Poetry of the Present

Modern poetry—that is to say, poems written in some sort of "free" form—does not put us off in the way of metrical poems. The writing of these poems seems like something we can do. The idiosyncratic and changeable form allows us to imagine that we can "imitate" it successfully: there are no apparent rules about it that we don't know and therefore cannot hope to use correctly. The familiarity of the language itself—not very different from the language that we use daily—gives confidence.* Also, many of the poems are short—if it is going to be difficult to write the poem, at least it can be done quickly!

Such confidence is helpful and will encourage students to plunge in rather than hang back. That's good. One learns by thinking about writing, and by talking about writing—but primarily through writing.

Imitating such poems is an excellent way to realize that they are not very similar after all, but contain differences that are constant, subtle, intense, and radiantly interesting. Let students try to imitate the spare

---

*Of course not all contemporary poets use language in this fairly accessible way. I am thinking of—and like to use as models—such poets as Robert Frost, Richard Eberhart, Theodore Roethke, Gwendolyn Brooks, Robert Hayden, Elizabeth Bishop, William Stafford, James Wright, John Haines, Denise Levertov, Donald Hall, Maxine Kumin, Lucille Clifton. This is by no means a complete list.

tenderness of a John Haines poem. Let them try the long cadences of Whitman, with their wonderful wrist-grip on physical delight and spiritual curiosity. Let them try to imitate Elizabeth Bishop, with her discerning and luminous eye. Let them attempt the fiery eruption of Robert Hayden or Linda Hogan, or the biting wisdom of Lucille Clifton. Let them imitate and imitate—and learn and learn.

Once again, one of the practices of visual arts students comes to mind as I write this: who has not seen a young painter in a museum intently copying a Vermeer, or a van Gogh, and believing himself on the way to learning something valuable?

Emotional freedom, the integrity and special quality of one's own work—these are not first things, but final things. Only the patient and diligent, as well as the inspired, get there.

Sound

To make a poem, we must make sounds. Not random sounds, but chosen sounds.

How much does it matter what kinds of sounds we make? How do we choose what sounds to make?

"Go!" does not sound like "Stop!" Also, in some way, the words do not *feel* the same. "Hurry up!" does not sound or feel like its opposite, "Slow down!" "Hurry up!" rustles with activity, leaps to its final punch. "Slow down!" pours from the tongue, as flat as two plates. Sounds differ. Sounds matter. "No ideas but in things," said William Carlos Williams. And, for our purposes here, no things but in the sounds of the words representing them. A "rock" is not a "stone."

But, why is a rock not a stone?

Dingdong, Onomatopoeia

The "dingdong" theory, not considered seriously anymore, remains intriguing. Here is Webster's* definition:

> A theory of Karl Wilhelm Heyse, supported (but later abandoned) by Max Müller. It maintains that the primitive elements of language are reflex expressions induced by sensory impressions; that is, the creative faculty gave to each general conception, as it thrilled for the first time through the brain, a phonetic expression;—so nicknamed from the analogy of the sound of a bell induced by the stroke of the clapper. . . . called also the bowwow theory, the poohpooh theory.

How disappointing that such a theory didn't survive! However, we still have *onomatopoeia,* individual sounds-tied-to-sense, which will be discussed later. But onomatopoeia does not extend across any great part of the language.

The Alphabet—Families of Sound

Let us look elsewhere then. What follows is from a textbook of grammar published in 1860.† It divides

---

*Webster's New International Dictionary of the English Language, Second Edition Unabridged (Springfield: G. & C. Merriam Company, 1958), pp. 20–21.
†This small, leather-bound volume by Goold Brown is Brown's Grammar, Improved (New York: The Institutes of English Grammar, 1860).
   It would be reasonable to suppose that I would reach for a more

the alphabet—our "raw material"—into various cate-
gories.

The letters are divided into two general
classes, *vowels* and *consonants*.

A vowel forms a perfect sound when uttered
alone. A consonant cannot be perfectly ut-
tered till joined to a vowel.

The vowels are *a, e, i, o, u,* and sometimes *w*
and *y*. All the other letters are consonants.

(*W* or *y* is called a consonant when it pre-
cedes a vowel heard in the same syllable, as in
wine, twine, whine. In all other cases these
letters are vowels, as in newly, dewy, and
eyebrow.)

The consonants are divided into *semivowels*
and *mutes*.

A semivowel is a consonant that can be im-
perfectly sounded without a vowel so that at
the end of a syllable its sound may be pro-
tracted, as *l, n, z,* in al, an, az.

---

modern text. On the day I looked into Brown's book, however, I wasn't
looking reasonably, but immediately; looking over titles in my own house,
my eye fell upon his book, and it was so instantly rich and provocative
that, for purposes of this discussion, I have stayed with it. I am not
trained in linguistics, and here I only want to make a few useful and
important points about sound.

The semivowels are *f, h, j, l, m, n, r, s, v, w,
x, y, z*, and *c* and *g* soft. But *w* or *y* at the end
of a syllable is a vowel. And the sound of *c, f,
g, h, j, s*, or *x* can be protracted only as an
aspirate, or strong breath.

Four of the semivowels—*l, m, n*, and *r*—are
termed *liquids*, on account of the fluency of
their sounds.

Four others—*v, w, y*, and *z*—are likewise
more vocal than the aspirates.

A mute is a consonant that cannot be
sounded at all without a vowel, and which
at the end of a syllable suddenly stops the
breath, as *k, p, t*, in ak, ap, at.

The mutes are eight: *b, d, k, p, q, t*, and *c* and
g hard. Three of these—*k, g*, and *c* hard—
sound exactly alike. *B, d*, and *g* hard stop the
voice less suddenly than the rest.

Here we begin to understand that our working mate-
rial—the alphabet—represents families of sounds rather
than random sounds. Here are mutes, liquids, aspi-
rates—vowels, semivowels, and consonants. Now we see
that words have not only a definition and possibly a
connotation, but also the *felt* quality of their own kind
of sound.

A Rock or a Stone

The following three phrases mean exactly the same thing. But we would use each of the phrases only under certain circumstances, and not at all under others. The phrases are:

1. Hush!
2. Please be quiet!
3. Shut up!

The first phrase we might use to quiet a child when we do not want to give any sense of disturbance or anger. (No mutes are here.)

The second phrase is slightly curt, but the tone remains civil. We might use it in a theater when asking strangers to stop talking. (This phrase makes use of four mutes—*p, b, q,* and *t,* but in almost every case the mute is instantly "calmed down," twice by a vowel and once by a liquid.)

The third phrase is the most curious and instructive. It is abrupt; it indicates, unarguably, impatience and even anger. Someone using this phrase means business. (In this phrase the mutes, *t* and *p,* are not softened; rather, the vowel precedes them; the mutes are the final brittle explosion of the word. Both words slap shut upon their utterance, with a mute.)

One group of phrases does not give conclusive evidence, but it does suggest that there is, or can be, a correlation between the meaning, connotation, and actual sound of the word.

Now, what is the difference between a rock and a

stone? Both use the vowel *o* (short in *rock,* long in *stone*), both are words of one syllable, and there the similarity ends. *Stone* has a mute near the beginning of the word that then is softened by a vowel. *Rock* ends with the mute *k*. That *k* "suddenly stops the breath." There is a seed of silence at the edge of the sound. Brief though it is, it is definite, and cannot be denied, and it feels very different from the *-one* ending of *stone.* In my mind's eye I see the weather-softened roundness of stone, the juts and angled edges of rock.

Robert Frost's
Stopping by Woods on a Snowy Evening

Read the poem *Stopping by Woods on a Snowy Evening,* by Robert Frost, keeping in mind exactly what is going on—the pause within a journey, the quiet, introspective voice of the speaker, the dark and solitary woods, the falling snow.

The initial four lines are rife with *w*'s and *th*'s; *f* is there, and *v.* Three sets of double *ll*'s. The heaviness of the vowels is increased by the use of diphthongs. The two words that end with a mute (*think* and *up*) are set within the lines and thus are softened. All other mutes are softened within the words themselves. One could scarcely read these lines in any other than a quiet, musing, almost whispered way.

One can say any number of things about the little horse of the second stanza. It is the only object in the poem on which the speaker focuses. It is the only other living thing in the poem, and it is as willing as the speaker for the moment is hesitant to continue the journey.

Stopping by Woods on a Snowy Evening
ROBERT FROST

Whose woods these are I think I know.
His house is in the village though;
He will not see me stopping here
To watch his woods fill up with snow.

My little horse must think it queer
To stop without a farmhouse near
Between the woods and frozen lake
The darkest evening of the year.

He gives his harness bells a shake
To ask if there is some mistake.
The only other sound's the sweep
Of easy wind and downy flake.

The woods are lovely, dark and deep.
But I have promises to keep,
And miles to go before I sleep,
And miles to go before I sleep.

In any case, we are drawn by the speaker to look at
the little horse too, and as we do so the sounds of
the whispery introduction, the interior monologue, no
louder than the snow falling, are interrupted with little
raps of sharper sound—not mallets, not that heavy, but
different. "My little horse must think it queer" is not a
very rattling line, but the sound of "think," with its
lightly snapping *k* this time followed not by a softer
sound but by the snippet "it," and "queer," an echo of
the *k,* makes it altogether livelier than the first stanza.
"Stop" is a rap of a sound, then it is quieted by the rest
of the line. After "lake" there is a momentary chasm, a
fracture of silence out of which a different kind of elec-
tricity flows before the line swings and the adjective
"darkest" repeats the *k* once more, two taps of disqui-
etude.

In stanza 3 the reversal has taken place. Instead of
the guttural mutes being quieted—swallowed up in a
plash of softer sounds—they rise up among and after
the soft sounds, insisting they be heard.

The first hard *g* in the poem occurs on the first
line of this third stanza: "he *gives* his harness bells a
shake. . . ." Though the *g* is instantly quieted by the
two *h*'s, the moment of introspection is almost over, and
the ear anticipates this with "bells" and with the word
"shake"—louder than "lake," more forceful. In the
following line the *k* repeats in the very meaningful
word "ask" (the traveler is not the only "asking" crea-
ture in the poem); and this line as well as the following
lines of the third stanza end with mutes. Altogether, in
this stanza, we have "shake," "mistake," "sweep," and
"flake," while, in the two stanzas preceding, there has

been only one such moment (the end word "lake" in line 7).

Something is stirring, in the very sound; it leads us to ready ourselves for the resolution in stanza 4. There, "the woods are lovely" takes us exactly back to the mood of the first stanza, but the second half of that line thumps out "dark and deep," both words beginning with a mute and ending with a mute. They represent, in the sound, themselves, and more than themselves. They say not only that the woods are dark and deep, but that the speaker has come to another place in his mind and can speak in this different way, designating with the voice, as with the gesture of an arm, a new sense of decision and resolution.

Line 2 of the last stanza both begins and ends with a mute, and there is the heavy *p* in "promises" in the center of the line. Lines 3 and 4, the same line repeated, are intricate indeed. "Miles," that soft sound, representative of all one's difficult mortal years, floats above the heavy mutes pacing to the end of the line—"go," "before," "sleep." The unmistakable, definite weights that are the mutes help to make the final line more than an echo of the third line. Everything transcends from the confines of its initial meaning; it is not only the transcendence in meaning but the sound of the transcendence that enables it to work. With the wrong sounds, it could not have happened.

I don't mean to suggest that Frost sat down and counted out the mutes, aspirates, etc., while writing the poem. Or that any poet does anything like this. I mean to suggest that poets select words for their sound as well as their meaning—and that good poets make good *initial* selections. Of course they also revise. But they have already—"naturally," one wants to say—worked from such a font of knowledge and sensitivity that often near-miracles of sound-and-sense have already happened.

How do they do this? Language aptitude differs from person to person, we know. Also, just as a brick-layer or any worker—even a brain surgeon—improves with study and experience, surely poets become more proficient with study and "practice."

Verbal skills *can* be learned. They can be discussed and practiced. Then, a wonderful thing happens: what is learned consciously settles, somewhere inside the chambers of the mind, where—you can count on it— it will "remember" what it knows and will *float forth to assist in the initial writing.*

Frost kept no jottings about sound while he wrote *Stopping by Woods on a Snowy Evening.* He did not need to. He was a master poet. The poem is an extraordinary statement of human ambivalence and resolution. Genius wrote it. But more than one technical device assisted, the first of which is an extraordinary use of sound.

More Devices
of Sound

A POEM ON THE PAGE speaks to the listening mind. Here are a few of the time-tested, enduring, and effective devices that have been used over and over. Each of them brightens the language and helps to hold the reader in thrall.

ALLITERATION, strictly speaking, is the repetition of the initial sound of words in a line or lines of verse.

When alliteration is well done, where is the line between enough and too much? Don't worry about excess. Practice this sonorous and lively device. Notice it in poems you read. Someday with the help of alliteration you may write lines as delicious (and excessive) as these, by Robert Penn Warren:

> The bear's tongue, pink as a baby's, out-crisps to
> the curled tip,

It bleeds the black blood of the blueberry.
>   (*Audubon: A Vision*)

Or these, by Robert Frost:

> I saw you from that very window there,
> Making the gravel leap and leap in air,
> Leap up, like that, like that, and land so lightly
> And roll back down the mound beside the hole.
>   (*Home Burial*)

Sometimes alliteration includes the repetition of both initial sounds and interior sounds of words, as in "blueberry." It is also, then, known as *consonance*. Here is an illustration:

> The little boy lost his shoe in the field.
> Home he hobbled, not caring, with a stick whip-
>   ping goldenrod.
>   (Robert Penn Warren,
>   *Little Boy and Lost Shoe*)

ASSONANCE is the repetition of vowel sounds within words in a line or lines of verse. In effect, such repetition creates a near-rhyme.

At the end of the passage from *Home Burial* just given to illustrate alliteration, there are three examples—three runs—of assonance (the first is marked with circles, the second with underlines):

@nd l@nd so lightly
@nd roll b@ck down the mound beside the hole.
(Robert Frost, *Home Burial*)

The coalitions *ow* in "down" and *ou* in "mound" constitute the third instance of assonance in this very brief
passage.

Because of its position inside words, assonance is
less obvious than alliteration, but this by no means implies that its effect is slight or unimportant. Another
example—a passage from a poem by May Swenson
titled *On Handling Some Small Shells from the Windward Islands*—follows:

Their scrape and clink
together of musical coin.

Then the tinkling of crickets
more eerie, more thin.

Their click as of crystal,
wood, carapace and bone.

A tintinnabular* fusion.
Their friction spinal and chill

In this run of short *i* sounds, the *i* used as part of a
diphthong (in "their," "coin," "eerie," and "fusion") is
not a part of the assonance proper; neither, of course,
is the long *i* in "spinal." But the *y* sound in the word
"crystal" is.

---

*Happily, she couldn't resist. (See the passage from Poe on the following
page.)

Yet it is reasonable to wonder whether the effect of the *i* sounds in the diphthongs, and most certainly the sudden sharp use of the long *i* in "spinal," are not a part of the total effect of the passage. In assonance, there are sibling sounds—also cousins, second cousins, etc.

ONOMATOPOEIA is the use of a word that, through its sound as well as its sense, represents what it defines. Frequently, though not always, such words are natural sounds. Bees *buzz,* for example, and cows *moo;* birds *chirp,* and thunder *rumbles.*

Edgar Allan Poe's poem *The Bells* has perhaps the most famous examples of onomatopoeia. Here are just four lines:

> Keeping time, time, time,
> In a sort of Runic rhyme,
> To the *tintinnabulation** that so musically wells
> From the bells, bells, bells, bells, . . .

"Tintinnabulation," that resonant noun, holds within it the very sound of the bells. Probably, though, more verbs than any other part of speech are employed onomatopoetically. Here are two more examples, both from poems by Robert Penn Warren:

> "We took the big bellied gun that *belched.* We broke it."
>
> (*Chief Joseph of the Nez Perce*)

---

*Italics mine in this and the following quotations.

In the cabin, a woman and her sons are drinking and whispering; Audubon lies awake and listens, and senses the threat to his life. Twice,

> He hears the *jug slosh*.

....

He hears the *jug slosh*.

> (*Audubon: A Vision*)

In each of these passages, of course, more than onomatopoeia is working toward the desired effect. In *The Bells*, rhythm supplies a sustaining part of the throbbing, bell-ringing atmosphere. In the second example, alliteration has an important preparatory role. In the third, the very brevity of the line, as well as the lack of any change or elaboration of the line, suggests how carefully Audubon had to listen, and how small the deadly sound must have been.

There is no name for the arrangement of vowel sounds, especially in the final line, of the following passage. Named or not, however, it is clear that the change or the interconnectedness of sound is an important matter.

> But the music of your talk
> Never shall the chemistry
> Of the secret earth restore.
> All your lovely words are spoken.
> Once the ivory box is broken,
> *Beats the golden bird no more.*

> (Edna St. Vincent Millay,
> *Memorial to D.C.: V. Elegy*)

Language is rich, and malleable. It is a living, vibrant material, and every part of a poem works in conjunction with every other part—the content, the pace, the diction, the rhythm, the tone—as well as the very sliding, floating, thumping, rapping sounds of it.

The Line

THE FIRST OBVIOUS DIFFERENCE between prose and poetry is that prose is printed (or written) within the confines of margins, while poetry is written in lines that do not necessarily pay any attention to the margins, especially the right margin.

The word *verse* derives from the Latin and carries the meaning "to turn" (as in *versus*). Poets today, who do not often write in the given forms, such as sonnets, need to understand what effects are created by the turning of the line at any of various possible points—within (and thus breaking) a logical phrase, or only at the conclusions of sentences, or only at the ends of logical units, etc.

This subject—turning the line—is one that every poet deals with throughout his or her working life. And gladly, too—for every turning is a meaningful decision, the effect of which is sure to be felt by the reader. This is so whether the poet is working in metrical forms or in free verse.

Discussion of the line, its power generally and the specific parts of that power, is best undertaken through an examination of the metric line, so that is how we will begin.

Length and Rhythm

Begin by considering (absorbing) the following four facts.

1. In metrical verse, each line of the poem can be divided into *feet,* and each foot into *stresses* (syllable sounds), to reveal the overall rhythmic pattern.

2. The process of dividing a line into its metrical feet and each foot into its individual parts is called *scansion.*

3. An *iamb,* or an *iambic foot,* is one light stress followed by one heavy stress. ˘ ´

EXAMPLE: Ŭpón

4. Five iambic feet strung together create an *iambic pentameter* line. ˘ ´ ˘ ´ ˘ ´ ˘ ´ ˘ ´

EXAMPLE: Ŭpón | thŏse bóughs | whĭch sháke | ăgaínst | thĕ cóld, . . .
      (William Shakespeare, *Sonnet LXXIII*)

The iambic pentameter (five foot) line* is the most widely used line in English metrical verse. This is the

---

*Other metrical lines, metrical feet, and the symbols used to indicate them, are given in the boxed material.

sonnet line; it is the line of Milton's *Paradise Lost,* of Shakespeare's plays and sonnets, of Wordsworth's *The Prelude.* It is also the line of many American poems, including many of the poems of Robert Frost.

Metrical Lines

1. A one-foot line is called *monometer.*
2. A two-foot line is called *dimeter.*
3. A three-foot line is called *trimeter.*
4. A four-foot line is called *tetrameter.*
5. A five-foot line is called *pentameter.*
6. A six-foot line is called *hexameter.* When it is a pure iambic line, it may be called an *alexandrine.*
7. A seven-foot line is called *heptameter.*
8. An eight-foot line is called *octameter.*

Metrical Feet and Symbols

1. *iamb:* a light stress followed by a heavy stress. ˘ ´
2. *trochee:* a heavy stress followed by a light stress. ´ ˘
3. *dactyl:* a heavy stress followed by two light stresses. ´ ˘ ˘
4. *anapest:* two light stresses followed by a heavy stress. ˘ ˘ ´
5. *spondee:* two equal stresses. – –

Here are a few *pentameter* lines that may be familiar
to you:

Forlorn! | the ver|y word | is like | a bell . . .
                    (John Keats, *To a Nightingale*)

Shall I | compare | thee to | a sum|mer's day?
                    (William Shakespeare, *Sonnet XVIII*)

The shat|tered wa|ter made | a mis|ty din.
Great waves | looked o|ver o|thers
     com|ing in, . . .
                    (Robert Frost, *Once by the Pacific*)

Bright star! | would I | were stead|fast as | thou
     art—
                    (John Keats, *Bright Star! Would I*
                    Were Steadfast as Thou Art)

Here are some *tetrameter* (four foot) lines, each con-
taining four light and four heavy stresses:

I wan|dered lone|ly as | a cloud
That floats | on high | o'er vales | and hills, . . .
          (William Wordsworth, *I Wandered Lonely* . . .)

In Xan|adu | did Ku|bla Khan
A state|ly plea|sure-dome | decree:
                    (Samuel Taylor Coleridge, *Kubla Khan*)

Whŏse woŏds | thĕse aŕe | Ĭ thínk | Ĭ knŏw.
Hĭs hoúse | ĭs ín | thĕ víl|lăge though; . . .

> (Robert Frost, *Stopping by Woods*
> *on a Snowy Evening*)

Though the difference in length is only a single foot,
pentameter and tetrameter are two quite different
things. In the tetrameter lines there is a sense of
quickness, spareness, even a little agitation, which is
not evoked in the five-foot lines (which are full, but
not over-full, without obvious pressure in any direc-
tion).

The *trimeter* (three foot) line can evoke an even
more intense sense of agitation and celerity:

Thĕ whís|kĕy ón | yŏur bréath
Coŭld máke | ă smáll | bŏy dízzў;
Bŭt Í | hŭng ón | lĭke déath:
Sŭch wál|tzĭng wás | nŏt éasў.

> (Theodore Roethke, *My Papa's Waltz*)

On the other side of the five-foot line lies the *hex-
ameter* or *alexandrine* (the first line is of course pen-
tameter; the second line is the alexandrine):

Ăwáke! | ărise! | mў lóve, | ănd féar|lĕss bé,
Fŏr o'ér | thĕ soúth|ĕrn moórs | Ĭ háve | ă
    hŏme | fŏr thée.

> (John Keats, *The Eve of St. Agnes*)

How important this choice of line length is! Its effect upon the reader is simple, reliable, and inescapable.

The *pentameter* line is the primary line used by the English poets not for any mysterious reason, but simply because the pentameter line most nearly matches the breath capacity of our English lungs—that is, speaking in English—and thus it is the line most free from any special effect.* It fits without stress, makes a full phrase, and leaves little breath at the end. It gives off, therefore, no particular message. It is, one might say, the norm.

All deviations from the norm do, however, emit messages. Excitement of all kinds, with its accompanying physical and psychic tension, "takes our breath." Any line shorter than pentameter indicates this. The reader is brought to a more than usual attentiveness by the shorter line, which indicates a situation in some way out of the ordinary. Tetrameter can release a felt agitation or restlessness, or gaiety, more easily and "naturally" than pentameter, and so on.

For when the prevailing mood is one of confidence and leisure, we take the time for length and breadth, going into details, nuance, even anecdotes perhaps. We might set a match to a pile of leaves, for example, and stand back and describe what happens in this manner. But when something is critical, painful, even worrisome, we have no time for such inessentials—should the bon-

---

*Of course even if this is so there must quickly have come into being historical and cultural influences as well—that is, once the pentameter line was established, and great works created in it, other poets coming along would naturally think to model their poems upon such a mighty form.

fire leap beyond our control, we would run from it, shouting the single word "Fire!" as we go.

The longer line (longer than five feet) suggests a greater-than-human power. It can seem by its simple endurance—beyond ordinary lung capacity—grandiose, prophetic. It can also indicate abundance, richness, a sense of joy. Underlying whatever freight of language (statement) it carries, it emits a sense of an unstoppable machine.

Robinson Jeffers's long lines often resonate with the feeling of prophecy, as does much of Whitman's work. Ginsberg's energy is often cradled appropriately in the lavishness of long lines.

In metrical verse, the lines may be all of the same length (number of feet), but in many cases the pattern includes lines of varying length, thus complicating the whole mechanism. The stanza (discussed in detail beginning on p. 60) generally used by Emily Dickinson (it is also the stanza form of the Protestant hymn, of much of Samuel Taylor Coleridge's *The Ancient Mariner,* as well as many other lyric poems) places a tetrameter line first followed by a trimeter line, then again a tetrameter and a trimeter. The foot (with occasional exceptions) is iambic, and frequently the phrasing holds through a two-line segment, as follows:

> Ĭt wás | nŏt Déath, | fŏr Í | stŏod úp,
> Ănd all | thĕ Déad, | lĭe dówn—
> Ĭt wás | nŏt Níght, | fŏr all | thĕ Bélls
> Pŭt oút | thĕir Tóngues, | fŏr Nóon.

(No. 510)

Even in this four-line passage, one can begin to no-
tice the many elements working toward the tone of
intensity so common in Dickinson's poems. A tetram-
eter line, agitating in itself, begins the piece. The
tension is increased by cutting the length of line two
by a foot and also by concluding the phrase begun
in line one within this shorter span. Then, a sim-
ilar two lines: tetrameter and trimeter again, creating
another single phrase. The repetition, so frequently
a device of pleasure, here evokes claustrophobia, a
sense of ritual—a terrible formality. One is reminded
of Dickinson's own phrase: "After great pain, a for-
mal feeling comes—" (from No. 341). Also, of course,
the sounds of the words are at work, and the simi-
larity of line-end sound (down / noon), and the breath-
lessness of the dash. Everything, that is, is at work
toward the effect of the piece—nothing is static, or
neutral.

Constancy

The reader, as he or she begins to read, quickly enters
the rhythmic pattern of a poem. It takes no more than
two or three lines for a rhythm, and a feeling of pleasure
in that rhythm, to be transferred from the poem to the
reader. Rhythm is one of the most powerful of pleasures,
and when we feel a pleasurable rhythm we hope it will
continue. When it does, the sweet grows sweeter. When
it becomes reliable, we are in a kind of body-heaven.
Nursery rhymes give this pleasure in a simple and won-
derful way.

This quick response to the prevailing rhythmic pattern is true of "free" verse as well as metrical verse, even though the pattern in free-form poems is less mathematically measurable than it is in metric verse.

Beginning writers need to remember how potent these patterns are. Rhythm underlies *everything*. Put one word on a line by itself in a poem of otherwise longish lines and, whether you mean it to be or not, it has become a critical word. All attention is drawn to it. It must mean something very important to be placed where it breaks the rhythm with such a slap and crack.

Alter the line length or the established rhythm when you want to, or need to, or choose to, to change the very physiological mood of the reader. Change the line length or rhythm arbitrarily, or casually, and you have puzzled and sensually irritated the reader— thrown him from his trance of interest and pleasure. And if pleasure is not an important function of the poem, why, I ask, did Wordsworth mention the word "pleasure" forty-two times in his *Preface to Lyrical Ballads?*

Of course when I speak of rhythm I don't mean a rhythm so strict or metronomic that it merely repeats itself exactly. Remember, language is a living material, full of shadow and sudden moments of up-leap and endless nuance. Nothing with language, including rhythmic patterns, should be or can be entirely exact and repetitious, nor would we like it if it were. Which brings us to the next subject, the necessary variations.

Variation

Lines of good poetry are apt to be a little irregular. A prevailing sense of rhythm is necessary, but some variation enhances the very strength of the pattern. The singsong poem is a dull poem.* Variation wakes us up with its touch of difference, just as a cadence of drums in a marching band keeps two things going at the same time: a strict and regular beat and a few contrapuntal accents, flourishes, even silences. This liveliness keeps us interested and "on our toes." Within the poem, irregularities may occur for the sake of variation; they may also occur because of stresses required by the words themselves, for accuracy, for emphasis, etc.

In addition, there may well be some variation between the way *I* read a line of a poem, and the way *you* read it. Neither of us has to be wrong; we may *both* be within the bounds of the reasonable. Perhaps it is partly this individual inflection with which each of us reads a poem that creates a personal bonding to it. It is a situation far more complicated, and interesting, than one in which only right or wrong is possible.

Look again at one of the lines offered as an example of iambic pentameter.

Forlorn! | the ver|y word | is like | a bell
                              (John Keats, *To a Nightingale*)

---

*But there is always the miraculous exception to the rule. *Stopping by Woods on a Snowy Evening* was written in regular iambic tetrameter—all sixteen lines, all sixty-four metric feet of it. Nuance and inflection provide the only variety.

In this line the regular pattern of iambic feet is scanned "correctly." And yet a reader of the line would surely make heavier stresses on the words "forlorn" and "bell" than on the words "very," "word," or "like," though each of these words too has a heavy accent. Clearly there are differing degrees of heavy and light stresses, under the rules of simple sense.

But there are lines in which clarity simply isn't brought forth sufficiently by this method of charging the light and heavy stresses differently. There are occasions when something more definite is called for. Consider these three lines from *Mr. Edwards and the Spider:*

> On Windsor Marsh, I saw the spider die
> When thrown into the bowels of fierce fire:
> ....
> Bŭt whó | căn plúmb | thĕ sínk|ĭng óf | thăt
> soúl?

> (Robert Lowell)

In the third line, the iambic pattern calls for a light stress on the word "that" in the final foot. But this makes no sense; the word itself, its meaning in the poem, calls for a heavy stress. Moreover, it seems entirely unacceptable to do anything in terms of pattern *or* sense with "soul" than to give it, too, a heavy stress.

There is accommodation to this kind of necessity; it is called the *spondee.* Two stresses, of equal weight, can replace the iambic foot in order to take care of compound words, such as "heartbreak," "breadboard," etc.—and at any time that logic or design calls for it. Thus the third line from the Lowell quotation can be

scanned as follows, and the phrase "that soul" be made
more readable:

> On Windsor Marsh, I saw the spider die
> When thrown into the bowels of fierce fire:
> ....
> Bŭt whŏ | căn plúmb| thĕ sínk | ĭng of | thăt
>   sōul?*

And consider one more line, that restrained outburst
from Keats:

> Bright stár! | woŭld Í | wĕre stéad|făst aś | thŏu
>   art—

The opening line of Keats's sonnet might also call for
some spondee replacement of the iambic pattern. I say
"might," for here is a case where it is difficult to say
that anything is right, or wrong. One could scan the line
as it appears in the beginning of this chapter, indicating
regular iambs. Or one might indicate a spondee at the
beginning of the line, so as to put equal weight upon
"bright" and "star":

> Brīght stār! | woŭld Í | wĕre stéad|făst aś | thŏu
>   art—

---

*The first line of this three-line passage is easy: straight iambs five times
over. Line 2 I offer to the reader for his or her own entanglement and
pleasure; "fierce fire" of course calls for the spondee, but what is one
to do with "bowels," and anyway is "bowels" one syllable or two syllables
here? I have *my* idea of it; readers will learn a lot by determining what
they think about it.

Additionally, one might prefer to read the word "stead-
fast" without lightening the second syllable, and so that
foot also could be scanned with a spondee:

> Bright star! | would I | were stead|fast as | thou
>   art—

Or, one might actually feel that, in this extraordinary
line, any light stress causes a loss of the personal and
immeasurable longing of the whole,* and so scan it as
follows:

> Bright star! | would I | were stead|fast as | thou
>   art—

I have explained previously why the pentameter part of
the iambic pentameter line is the most widely used line
in the English language—because its length matches the
breath capacity of our lungs. The iambic foot has wide
currency for a similar "natural" reason. It is the para-
mount sound in any string of English words, thus it is
the most fluid, the most uncontrived sounding meter.
Phrases falling naturally into the iambic pattern are no-
ticeable in every kind of writing. Compared to it, any
other meter, in fact, sounds "composed"—not unlike
one of those snapping flourishes of the drums.

---

*Also, it is easy to see that any change from the regular pattern causes
a disturbance along the rest of the line—now it is clear that the light
stress on "thou" has become awkward, and that foot by itself at least
would require a spondee, had I not elected at this point to scan the
entire line with spondees.

This is the opening line of *Mending Wall* by Robert Frost:

Sŏmethĭng | thĕre ís | thăt dóes|n't lóve|ă
wáll, . . .

The first foot of the line is the opposite of the iambic foot—the heavy stress comes first and is followed by a light stress. This is called a *trochee*. It is a wonderful and forceful way to begin a line.* It can be used anywhere within a line also, replacing an iambic foot. Or, it may be the prevailing line, as in this familiar passage from Shakespeare's *MacBeth:*

Dóublĕ, dóublĕ toíl ănd tróublĕ;
Fírĕ, búrn; ănd, cáuldrŏn, búbblĕ.

Another meter, which can replace the iamb or the trochee, or may be used as the prevailing pattern, is the *dactyl*. The word *happiness* is a dactyl—one heavy stress followed by two light stresses. *Dactyl* comes from a

---

*You may have noticed and wondered about the initial trochee foot in passages quoted on the previous pages. One appears in the passage quoted from Blake, another in one of the passages quoted from Keats.

It is fascinating to see when Frost uses the iamb to begin a poem and when he chooses the trochee or dactyl. More often than not he uses an iamb when the poem begins with narration, and a trochee or dactyl (the more formal, "composed" sound) when the poem starts with dialogue. Often in these poems the first word is a person's name or a place name. See *The Witch of Coös, Death of a Hired Man, A Hundred Collars,* etc.

Greek stem meaning finger—one long finger bone fol-
lowed by two short finger bones.

Here is a well-known example of the dactylic pat-
tern, from the poem *Evangeline:*

> Thĭs ĭs thĕ |forést prĭ|mévăl. Thĕ | múrmŭrĭng
> | pínĕs ănd thĕ | hémlŏcks,
> Béardĕd wĭth | móss, ănd ĭn | gármĕnts | gréen,
>   ĭndĭs|tínct ĭn thĕ | twílĭght,
> Stánd lĭke | Drúĭds ŏf | éld, wĭth | vóicĕs | sád
>   ănd prŏ|phétĭc, . . .

(Henry Wadsworth Longfellow)

And here is an example of dactylic meter used within
a poem whose pattern is not at all constant, but changes
from one kind of metric foot to another, elevating and
intensifying the poem's tone and meaning:

> Lĕt lóv|ĕrs gŏ frésh | ănd swéet | tŏ bé |
>   ŭndóne,
> Ănd thĕ | héavĭĕst | núns wālk | ĭn ă púre |
>   flóatĭng |
> Ŏf dárk | hábĭts, |
>   kéepĭng thĕir | díffĭcŭlt |
> bálănce.

(Richard Wilbur, *Love Calls Us
to the Things of This World*)

The *anapest* is the opposite of the dactyl, two light
stresses followed by a heavy stress. It is fairly uncommon.

And yet you see it used in the preceding quotation, and here are two lines that are probably familiar:

> For thĕ moón | nĕvĕr beáms | wĭthoŭt brińg |
> ĭnǵ mĕ dreáms
> Of thĕ beáu|tĭfŭl Ánn|ăbĕl Leé;
>
> (Edgar Allan Poe, Annabel Lee)

It is important to remember that all of these meters are terms for rhythmic patterns. They may be "pure" or they may have some variation and be "impure." Nursery rhymes are full of "impure" anapestic and dactylic lines—they use the metric patterns, but tend to end each line with a single heavy stress, as in

> "Híckŏrў | dĭckŏrў | doćk. | Thĕ moúse | răn
> úp | thĕ cloćk."

Consider the interior of the metrical line; there is a particularly effective device that can break into the established tempo of the line, thereby indicating—almost announcing—an important or revelatory moment. It is called the *caesura*. It is a structural and logical pause within and only within the line, and usually, but not always, within a metrical foot itself.

The pause is not counted as part of the metrical pattern.

> Fŏrlorń! | ↓ thĕ vér|ў wórd | ĭs lĭke | ă béll
>
> (John Keats, To a Nightingale)

In his exceedingly thoughtful essay about this poem,* Archibald MacLeish suggests it is here—at this very point—that the poem turns and the speaker determines not to follow the magical bird, but to return to earthly matters.

The way in which different poets use the caesura is almost a signature of their poetic style. In the four lines by Emily Dickinson previously quoted (see p. 41), a sense of hesitation, even claustrophobia (her breathlessness, her anxiety, as indicated by the short phrases), is heightened by the momentary but definite grip of the commas that hold back the last part of each line for just an instant, as if, in each case, they required a second push.

The caesura is useful not only where emotion is amassed, but in such lines as these, which set a conversational tone, at the beginning of *West-Running Brook:*

> "Fred, where is north?" ↓
>
>   "North? ↓ North is
> there, my love.
> The brook runs west. . . ."
>
>   (Robert Frost)

There *is* an uncounted stress. It is the final light stress of words that rhyme on double syllables. An example appears in the quotation from Theodore Roethke's poem *My Papa's Waltz* (see p. 39), in which there is an

---

*Archibald MacLeish, *Poetry and Experience* (Boston: Houghton Mifflin, 1960), pp. 173–99.

extra light syllable in the final foot of line 2, and again in line 4, deriving from the second syllables of the rhyming words "dizzy" and "easy." Such an extra light stress within a final foot is commonly called a *tag* and is not counted as part of the metrical pattern.

But the matter of rhyme is properly a subject of the following section.

The Beginning of the Line and the End of the Line

The most important point in the line is the *end* of the line. The second most important point is the *beginning* of it.

More poems begin with iambic meter than any other construction. The mood is relaxed, invitational—natural. Robert Frost would begin to read a poem so directly after making a personal remark, and the iambic line was so natural, that it was sometimes difficult to tell just where his "talk" ended and the poem began.

When a poem does begin with a heavy stress (spondee, trochee, or dactyl in metrical verse), it immediately signals to the reader that something dramatic is at hand. Something different from ordinary speech.

We all know what rhyme is.

When the stars threw down their spears
And water'd heaven with their tears,
Did He smile His work to see?
Did He who made the lamb make thee?

(William Blake, The Tyger)

The similarity of sound at the end of two or more lines creates cohesion, order, and gives pleasure. Obvious rhyme is *meant* to be noticed and to please. In fact, the mood of rhyming poems is often lighthearted.*

The rhyme occurring on the words "spears" and "tears" is called *true rhyme*. It is also a *masculine rhyme:* the words rhyme on a single stressed syllable.

When the words are not true rhyming words (like *pot* and *hot*) but almost rhyme (like *down* and *noon* in the Emily Dickinson quotation on p. 41) it is called *off-rhyme,* or *slant rhyme*. And *feminine rhyme* uses words of more than one syllable that end with a light stress, as in "buckle" and "knuckle." The rhyme on lines 2 and 4 of the Roethke stanza (p. 39) is an example of both slant rhyme and feminine rhyme.

Feminine endings tend to blur the end rhyme. So does slant rhyme. Masculine and true rhyme endings are forthright. And masculine true rhymes with words ending in mute sounds are the most emphatic rhymes of all—they slam the gate shut. Consider the last stanza of Frost's poem *Stopping by Woods on a Snowy Evening* (p. 25).

The repetition of lines, or the use of a refrain line, is a source of enjoyment. Both evoke the old pleasure of things occurring and reoccurring—rhythm, in fact.

After a repetition or a refrain, the reader, given the pattern clue that the next lines are obviously going to be different, is prone to listen to them with more than ordinary attention.

---

*But not always. You can't get more serious than Blake.

Turning the Line

Always, at the end of each line there exists—inev-
itably—a brief pause. This pause is part of the motion
of the poem, as hesitation is part of the dance. With it,
the poet working with metrical verse can do several
things, as indicated above. In addition, apart from the
length of line and the requirements of the meter, the
poet must decide where within the phrase itself to turn
the line over.

The writer of nonmetrical verse also has this end-
of-the-line pause to work with and can choose among
various ways of handling it. Say the writer chooses to
make the line self-enclosed. A *self-enclosed* line may be
an entire sentence, or it may be a phrase that is complete
in terms of grammar and logic, though it is only a part
of a sentence. In such a case—in Ezra Pound's poem
Salutation, for example—the pause works as an instant
of inactivity, in which the reader is "invited" to weigh
the information and pleasure of the line.

When, on the other hand, the poet *enjambs* the
line—turns the line so that a logical phrase is inter-
rupted—it speeds the line for two reasons: curiosity
about the missing part of the phrase impels the reader
to hurry on, and the reader will hurry twice as fast over
the obstacle of a pause because it is there. We leap with
more energy over a ditch than over no ditch.

Turning the line, in free verse, is associated not only
with the necessary decision at each turn (since the poem
is not following any imposed order), but it also has much
to do with the visual presentation on the page. Free

Salutation

EZRA POUND

O generation of the thoroughly smug
    and thoroughly uncomfortable,
I have seen fishermen picnicking in the sun,
I have seen them with untidy families,
I have seen their smiles full of teeth
    and heard ungainly laughter.
And I am happier than you are,
And they were happier than I am;
And the fish swim in the lake
    and do not even own clothing.

verse came into fashion just as the availability of books was becoming widespread, and the practice of reading poems with one's eyes, and listening to them silently, was taking precedence over the oral tradition. The pattern on the page, then, became the indicator of pace, and the balance and poise of the poem was inseparable from the way the line breaks kept or failed a necessary feeling of integrity, a holding together of the poem from beginning to end. The regular, metrical line gave assistance to a listener who sought to remember the poem; the more various line breaks of the "visual" poem gave assistance to the mind seeking to "hear" the poem.

Conclusion

No two poems will sound exactly alike, even though both are written in, say, iambic tetrameter rhyming couplets. Every poem has a basic measure, and a continual counterpoint of differences playing against that measure. Poems that do not offer such variations quickly become boring. The gift of words—their acute and utter wakefulness—is drowned in a rhythm that is too regular, and the poem becomes, instead of musical, a dull and forgettable muttering.

On the other hand, the poem needs to be reliable. I cannot say too many times how powerful the techniques of line length and line breaks are. You cannot swing the lines around, or fling strong-sounding words, or scatter soft ones, to no purpose. A reader beginning a poem is like someone stepping into a rowboat with a stranger at the oars; the first few draws on the long oars

through the deep water tell a lot—is one safe, or is one
apt to be soon drowned? A poem is that real a journey.
Its felt, reliable rhythms can invite, or can dissuade. A
meaningful rhythm will invite. A meaningless rhythm
will dissuade.

Some
Given Forms

A POEM REQUIRES A DESIGN—a sense of orderliness. Part of our pleasure in the poem is that it is a well-made thing—it gives pleasure through the authority and sweetness of the language *used in the way that it is used*. Even if the poem is a description of unalleviated chaos, it is a gathering of words and phrases and patterns that have been considered, weighed, and selected. Perhaps the poem was conceived in raw genius. It was also drawn through the measured strings of the man-made harp of song.

In the chosen design, all of the things talked about in the previous chapters are important—rhyme, meter, length of line, and the sounds of the various letters. Other things matter too, including the overall length of the poem, its tone (elevated or casual, for example), the extent to which imagery* is used, the subject itself. Be-

---

*An upcoming chapter focuses on imagery.

cause there are so many elements in the design of each poem, a pattern may be repeated but will not, in fact, cause one poem to be more than roughly like another. No two poems are alike, not anywhere in the world, at any time, nor will they ever be.

The following are brief descriptions of some of the patterns used in metrical verse.

Length, Breadth, and Rhyme

Rhyming patterns include everything from simple rhyming *couplets* (line 1 rhymes with line 2, line 3 rhymes with line 4, and so forth) to the *terza rima* and the *Spenserian stanza*.

Here are a few rhyming patterns:*

Couplet	*aa bb cc dd*, etc.
Tercet, or Triplet	*aaa bbb ccc ddd*, etc.
Quatrain	*abab cdcd*, etc.
Terza Rima	*aba bcb cdc ded*, etc.
Spenserian Stanza	*abab bcbc c†*

The *sonnet* is a poem of fourteen lines; traditionally it uses the iambic pentameter line, although poets have

---

*There are many additional forms and patterns; the interested reader will have no difficulty discovering them.

†In the Spenserian stanza, the first eight lines are always iambic pentameter; the final line is always an alexandrine (the six-foot line).

Of course, in most patterns of rhyme the poet may choose line length. For example, the poet might choose pentameter couplets, or quatrains in tetrameter, or make up a "new" design—note the rhyming pattern of *Stopping by Woods on a Snowy Evening*.

written sonnets in tetrameter, or in some other way varied the pure form.

The *Italian sonnet* uses the following rhyming scheme:

> *abba abba cdd cee*
> (other variations of *cde* are permissible)

The first eight lines (the *octave*) set out a statement or premise; the following six lines (the *sestet*) respond to it.

The *English* or *Shakespearean sonnet* is slightly less tight. Its rhyme scheme is as follows:

> *abab cdcd efef gg*

The English sonnet divides into three quatrains and a final couplet.

Poems written in iambic pentameter without end rhyme are called *blank verse*. The list of poems written in blank verse is practically endless; it includes *Hamlet, Doctor Faustus, Paradise Lost, Hyperion, The Prelude, Tinturn Abbey, The Second Coming, Death of a Hired Man,* and many, many others.

The Stanza

Stanza is the term by which we designate a group of lines in a poem that is separated by an extra amount of space from other groups of lines, or other stanzas. The word comes from the Latin (*stans,* present participle of *stare,* to stand) and through the Italian (*stanza,* a room or habitation). While it is clear that the term is used to indicate the divisions of the poem, there is no further *exact* definition. There are no absolutely right or wrong ways to divide a poem into stanzas, except, of course, when one is following a pattern that includes a particular strict formation of stanzas and stanza breaks.

It may be useful, when considering the stanza, to recall the paragraph in prose, which indicates a conclusion of one thought and the beginning of another, a *sensible* division. I don't mean that the poet should necessarily use the stanza in this way, or this way only, but that the poet might think of the sensible paragraph as a kind of norm (as the iambic pentameter line is a norm in terms of line-length expressiveness) from which to feel out the particular divisions that are best for a particular poem. Such divisions might be natural pauses in the action which is going on in the poem, or they might well be based on something else.

It can be said with certainty that a stanza break will inevitably result in either a felt hesitation or a felt acceleration. Ending a stanza at the end of a sentence strengthens the natural pause that follows any line and any completed sentence. Running a sentence through a final line of one stanza and on into the first line of the next stanza hastens the tempo, sometimes extraordinarily. Additionally, it can create a feeling of creative power (power of subject, power of poet) over mere neatness.

Any change from an established pattern indicates that the poet wants the reader to feel something different at that point. One of the assets of a pattern is this ability to "manipulate" the reader by breaking it.

Besides being a guide to the way the poet wants the reader to feel and understand the poem, each stanza is a part of the design of the poem—a part of its formal order. The stanza is therefore a pleasurable as well as a useful thing.

A poem may also be divided into different sections, numbered or not, and such divisions within a single poem do not need to follow any formal pattern. Rather they may travel wherever the particular requirements of the poem lead the poet. It is difficult in the usual single-bodied poem to break away from those two ordinary entities attached to any ongoing narrative—I mean time and place—even though such breaking-away to some-thing else might sharpen and deepen the context of the poem. With the use of separate sections, however, the poet may change the landscape, the narrative, the tone of the writing, line length—in fact, anything and every-thing. This is not to say that the poem does not require its focus and sequential unfolding, but rather that the poet is free to present material with a sort of wheeling complexity—as James Wright does in *Before a Cashier's Window in a Department Store*—unencumbered by the formality and implicit margins of the more formal poem.

Syllabic Verse

After all the talk about meter and stresses, here is some-thing quite different. In syllabic verse, a pattern is set up, and rigorously followed, in which the number of syllables in each of the lines of the first stanza is exactly repeated in the following stanzas. Whether the words on the various lines are words of single syllables or words

Before a Cashier's Window
in a Department Store
JAMES WRIGHT

1

The beautiful cashier's white face has risen
    once more
Behind a young manager's shoulder.
They whisper together, and stare
Straight into my face.
I feel like grabbing a stray child
Or a skinny old woman
And driving into a cellar, crouching
Under a stone bridge, praying myself sick,
Till the troops pass.

2

Why should he care? He goes.
I slump deeper.
In my frayed coat, I am pinned down
By debt. He nods,
Commending my flesh to the pity of the
    daws of God.

3

Am I dead? And, if not, why not?
For she sails there, alone, looming in the
    heaven of the beautiful.
She knows
The bulldozers will scrape me up
After dark, behind
The officers' club.

Beneath her terrible blaze, my skeleton
Glitters out. I am the dark. I am the dark
Bone I was born to be.

4

Tu Fu woke shuddering on a battlefield
Once, in the dead of night, and made out
The mangled women, sorting
The haggard slant-eyes.
The moon was up.

5

I am hungry. In two more days
It will be spring. So this
Is what it feels like.

of multiple syllables does not matter. Neither does it matter where the stresses fall in the individual lines. What matters is that the syllable *count* of each line, in each stanza, be exactly repeated; thus is the pattern set.

Because of the strictness of syllable-count, and the inevitable variety of stress-pattern, syllabic verse creates a music that is highly regular and at the same time filled with engaging counterpoint. Here is an example, from Marianne Moore's poem *The Fish*.

The Fish
wade
through black jade.
    Of the crow-blue mussell-shells, one keeps
    adjusting the ash-heaps:
        opening and shutting itself like

an
injured fan.
    The barnacles which encrust the side
    of the wave, cannot hide
        there for the submerged shafts of the

sun,
split like spun
    glass, move themselves with spotlight swiftness
    into the crevices—

In other words, in each stanza: line 1 has one syllable, line 2 has three syllables, line 3 has nine syllables, line 4 has six syllables, and line 5 has eight syllables, and there is no change in this pattern.

Again, a syllabic pattern is established by the exact repetition of the syllable-count. In *The Fish,* Moore has chosen to indent some of the lines, but not all of the lines. She has employed the title of the poem as a part of the opening sentence, and she has chosen to enjamb some lines and to end-stop others and to include rhyme. The syllabic regularity makes it syllabic verse, the rest is simply more design—a design which, by its variety, by the slippery entering of the title into text, and by loosening lines from the torpor of the usual frozen left margin, gives to the poem a quickened dose of motion, which is pleasurable.

One final note. Marianne Moore's poem *The Steeple-Jack,* also in syllabic verse, has, at its center, one wonderfully effective variant stanza. Invention hovers always a little above the rules.

Free Verse

The free verse poem is by no means exempted from the necessity of having a design, though one must go about it in rather different ways, since there is no external pattern to be followed. This subject will take up a fair amount of time in the following chapter, and will involve such matters as repetition of line, repetition of syntax, patterns of stress, a sense of inevitability, setting up a felt pattern of expectation and meeting that expectation, a repetition of enjambment, and so on.

Verse
That Is Free

Design

The name itself—free verse—implies that this kind of poetry rose out of a desire for release from the restraints of meter, the measured line, and strict rhyming patterns. Other terms are used to indicate this kind of verse also—the "fluid" poem, the "organic" poem. Each of the terms tries, but not very successfully, to say just what this kind of poetry is. The second and third terms are closer to the truth than "free verse"; still, "free verse" is the term most widely used.

Free verse is not, of course, free. It is free from formal metrical design, but it certainly isn't free from some kind of design. Is poetry language that is spontaneous, impulsive? Yes, it is. Is it also language that is composed, considered, appropriate, and effective, though you read the poem a hundred times? Yes, it is. And this is as true of free verse as it is of metrical verse.

No one, however, can say just exactly what the free-verse design is. Partly because it is so different from one poem to another. Partly because we are so close to the beginnings of it. Metrical verse has been written for centuries, and, before that, poetry depended on strict application of alliteration or some pattern of light and heavy stresses. Poets began to write free verse near the beginning of this century. Free verse is still in its developmental stages, then. The rules are not yet set in stone, or even in clay. Discussing free verse is like talking about an iceberg, a shining object that is mostly underwater.

The free-verse poem sets up, in terms of sound and line, a premise or an expectation, and then, before the poem finishes, it makes a good response to this premise. This is the poem's design. What it sets up in the beginning it sings back to, all the way, attaining a *felt* integrity.

The initial premise is made up of everything the old metrical premise is composed of—sound, line length, and rhythm patterns, but in this case they are not strict, they are not metrical. They do, however, make emphatic use of stresses, as speech does. Is speech not musical too? It is, indeed, and many of the old devices, such as refrain and repetition, are therefore still effective. Alliteration and assonance are as important as ever.

This much is certainly true: the free-verse poem, when finished, must "feel" like a poem—it must be an intended and an effective presentation. It need not scan, but it may scan a little if the poet is so inclined. It need not rhyme in a definite pattern, but it may rhyme a little, if the poet decides to rhyme a little. It need not follow particular stanza formations, though of course it *may* have stanzas. It need not follow any of the old rules, *necessarily*. Neither does it have to avoid all of them, *necessarily*.

Tone and Content

Perhaps free verse was a product of the times. Perhaps it resulted from a desire on the part of writers at the beginning of this century to alter the *tone* of the poem. Perhaps it had something to do with the increasing idea of a democratic and therefore classless society in America. Perhaps the proliferation of privately owned books had something to do with a changed attitude toward literature in general, and the poem in particular. As small towns and farming settlements grew into the west, with their distance from and independence from tradition, the idea of author-as-lecturer, as a member of an educated, special class, was scarcely applicable. Now the poet was being called down from the lectern and invited, as it were, into the privacy of each reader's home. The poet was expected to be more friendly— less "teacherly." Content began to change. The slight glaze of gentility, and the ever-present question of the suitability of the subject matter faded into the background. The emerging voice, it seemed, was determined to write about anything and everything. With such expectations—of intimacy, of "common" experience—the old metrical line, formal and composed, must have seemed off-putting. A new tone, reflecting this growing relationship between writer and reader, was called for.

In order for the tone of the poem to change, the line had to change. Now a line was needed that would sound and feel not like formal speech but like conversation. What was needed was a line which, when read, would feel as spontaneous, as true to the moment, as talk in the street, or talk between friends in one's own house.

This line naturally would have to affiliate itself more with the iambs and dactyls of natural speech patterns —the forward-reaching feeling of speech—than with the measures of meter. That, I think, is the long and the short of it. Speech entered the poem. The poem was no longer a lecture, it was time spent with a friend. Its music was the music of conversation.

Walt Whitman and *Leaves of Grass*

Walt Whitman, whose *Leaves of Grass* was first published in 1855, wrote almost all of his work in long, unscannable, usually end-stopped lines,* and he is frequently cited as the first American poet to write in free verse. It is like calling a mountain a hill. It isn't wrong. But it tells us nothing useful or interesting. Whitman's work—colossal, unique—is fairly categorized as free verse now that free verse has been invented. But to study Whitman's poetry is to learn about Whitman's poetry. Such is genius. In the sense that he broke with tradition, and was a celebrant of things American, and a talker, and an iconoclast, he serves as the vanguard to all that comes after. But the effect of his own work—with its

---

O Captain! My Captain! however, is written in meter, and is a fairly miserable poem.

From *Leaves of Grass*

WALT WHITMAN

I think I could turn, and live with animals,
    they are so placid and self-contain'd,
I stand and look at them long and long.

They do not sweat and whine about their
    condition,
They do not lie awake in the dark and weep
    for their sins,
They do not make me sick discussing their
    duty to God,
Not one is dissatisfied, not one is demented
    with the mania of owning things,
Not one kneels to another, nor to his kind that
    lived thousands of years ago,
Not one is respectable or unhappy over the
    whole earth.

extremely long lines; its repetitions, catalogs; its plen-
titude of adjectives, which would probably be death in
anyone else's work—is the result of an extremely per-
sonal style. Additionally, his tone—rhetorical, oratori-
cal—misses exactly what free verse, in its attitude and
tone, was setting out to do.

William Carlos Williams and *The Red Wheelbarrow*

If there is any single poem that might serve as a "text"
for a discussion of free verse, it must be William Carlos
Williams's poem *The Red Wheelbarrow*. This eight-line
poem has passed through endless scrutiny, and still it
refuses to give up all its secrets. But it does tell us a
great deal.

To begin with, it lies upon the page in a careful
visual pattern—four two-line stanzas. In each case the
second line of the stanza is a single word. And there is
no punctuation.

What does this design mean? What does it mean
that there is no punctuation? Perhaps the lack of punc-
tuation is trying to say that this is a new kind of poem,
to be read in a new way—taking clues from the very
graphic layout itself—from the line breaks primarily,
rather than the old formalities of comma or dash.

What does its apparent simplicity mean? Perhaps
that for this writer a poem is not a matter of some serious
predetermined subject, but of concentrated focus and
attention upon an "ordinary" simple subject—a mere
scene—then, through the elevation of art, the scene is

The Red Wheelbarrow
WILLIAM CARLOS WILLIAMS

so much depends
upon

a red wheel
barrow

glazed with rain
water

beside the white
chickens

lifted into the realm of something quite extraordinary and memorable.

What does it mean that this short poem is full of objects rather than ideas or thoughts? Williams said, "no ideas but in things." The idea springs from the object, then. The poem is not a discussion, not a lecture, but an *instance*—an instance of attention, of noticing something in the world.

What does it mean that the poem is so brief—only eight lines? Perhaps that such intense focus can't hold for any great length, or must break and move on to another object—another scene, another group of *things*. Perhaps Williams is implying that the imagination comes alive in the world of things—of objects. Perhaps he is saying that the poem, to become radiant, needs images, and images always involve things.

In terms of the sound of the poem, it is quickly apparent that the poem makes brilliant use of dark, heavy mutes. They appear in one important place after another, just as they did in Frost's poem *Stopping by Woods on a Snowy Evening*. Forget for a moment where the heavy stresses would come in speech and allow a heavy stress to fall upon those syllables constructed of or containing a mute and only upon those syllables. Then, speak the poem, stressing those points—and you are speaking in the natural pattern of speech. That is, the use of mutes and speech-stress work exactly as one force. And the sentence, fortified by these two sources of energy, becomes astonishingly forceful, unarguable, unforgettable.

Enjambment—as I have said before—gives the writer an ability to restrain or to spur on the pace of the poem. Like everything else about writing poems, the device of enjambment has about it a great flexibility; it can be employed in many ways, and it can work upon the reader to varying degrees. A line may be a grammatical whole, a sentence, or at least a logical unit. Or a phrase of logic may be broken entirely. Or a logical phrase may be broken at an apparently sensible point, letting the reader feel satisfaction at the end of the line; then, the following line may deliver some continuing information which redevelops the previous line. Sometimes this information is merely continuing, sometimes it is surprising. Two of the stanzas in this poem develop in this way, with the phrases "a red wheel" and "glazed with rain" redeveloping into "a red wheel / barrow" and "glazed with rain / water." It is fun. It is a world forming as we read. It is a poem that happens before our eyes.

Enjambment *can* be serious, disruptive, almost painful. In *The Red Wheelbarrow* it is none of these. Still, it is the main machinery of the poem, and sets the tone of the poem. The varying states of satisfaction and curiosity at the ends of the lines are deft and engaging. They keep us alert. Through them, the poem is unwrapped little by little, like paper pulled back from something sweet: a small, perfectly focused picture which—amazing!—has been created entirely from words and which—amazing!—we see so clearly at the end of the poem and which—amazing!—*we see ourselves seeing so clearly*. It is, above all, a poem that celebrates not only a momentary enchantment plucked out of the vast world but the deftness and power of the imagination and its dazzling material: language.

Diction,
Tone, Voice

"WATCH YOUR LANGUAGE!" you say to someone
who has just expressed himself with the help of slang
or an expletive. What you really mean is "Watch your
diction!" *Diction* means word choice.

The overall effect of the diction of a piece of writing,
in addition to other elements, such as choice of subject,
imagery, design of the poem, etc., is called *tone*.

The term *voice* is used to identify the agency or agent
who is speaking through the poem, apart from those
passages that are actual dialogue. This voice, or speaker
of the poem, is often called the *persona*.

The Contemporary Poem

For a poet, and indeed for any writer, diction has several
components—the *sound* of the word; the *accuracy* of
the word; and its *connotation*—the atmosphere, let us
say, that is created by word choice.

Matters of sound were discussed in an earlier chapter. And we hardly need to dwell on the requirement of accuracy in the language of the poem, I hope! Which gives us leave to turn directly to the third factor, connotation.

As I have indicated, the body of poetry from which American poetry developed carried with it a sense of formality, of *difference* from the ordinary world. Metrical construction was part of it. An *intended* formality was another part of it.

Much of contemporary poetry—though by no means all of it—is written in a diction that almost belies that it was formally composed: its general tone is one of natural and friendly intimacy; the language is not noticeably different from ordinary language. You find words that are neither pretentious nor especially formal. They try to make the poem clear and accessible.

And you find the words of the poems placed in a rather uncomplicated order—rather the way you use words yourself, in fact. You find a style that is neither elaborate, nor prepossessing, nor self-conscious, nor rhetorical. You find that most of the poems are gatherings of words, in good order, in *simple* order, plain and appealing.

Very likely the mood that develops between you and such poems is one of confidence, even intimacy. You feel that the poems might have been written to you. They are not unlike letters you might have received from a good friend.

This tone of intimacy, of course, didn't just happen. It happened because the writer intended for it to happen. And while this is by no means the only kind of

"i am accused of tending to the past . . ."
LUCILLE CLIFTON

i am accused of tending to the past
as if i made it,
as if i sculpted it
with my own hands. i did not.
this past was waiting for me
when i came,
a monstrous unnamed baby,
and i with my mother's itch
took it to breast
and named it
History.
she is more human now,
learning language every day,
remembering faces, names and dates.
when she is strong enough to travel
on her own, beware, she will.

poetry being written by contemporary poets, it is certainly one of the major styles, arguably *the* main style. Inside this poem of plain speech, the poet has moved, with great skill and all deliberate speed, from the role of "professor" to the role of fellow-citizen, neighbor, and friend.

And so there exists a definite sense of a *person,* a perfectly *knowable* person, behind the poem. In truth, it often seems that part of the poem's raison d'être is precisely to give us information about the writer— whether or not these facts are actual—even sometimes to tell the reader the most intimate details of the writer's life.

I don't suggest here that such a style of writing is either good or bad, only that it exists—that it is a common style of our time. It is the kind of poem the beginning writer is very likely to read, and thus to imitate.

I do suggest that there are two very possible consequences of this "knowable" person behind the poem. It may well be this sense of the poet—previously a rather mysterious and removed figure—as an ordinary, "knowable" person that has encouraged so many people to hope that they too can write poems. This new concept of the poet is invitational, and the spirit of our times is participatory, after all.

Also, I have wondered if the availability of this poem "format"—the poem as a candid and revelatory document—wasn't a timely encouragement to people to speak out about their personal and community life, to reveal themselves, as it were. I am speaking of women writers, and Afro-American writers, and Native Amer-

ican writers, for example, whose poems are often elo-
quent and powerful disclosures of gender or ethnic
truths. I don't mean that this is all there is to it by any
means; any innovation in a literary field must take fire
from many sparks in the societal atmosphere. But it is
a curious and even a marvelous fact: just at a time when
these voices passionately wished to speak out, there was
a poem-style that, in terms of apparatus and mood, was
suitable for the purpose, and so seemingly plain and
simple that it could, and I believe did, encourage many
people who would never have attempted more formal
verse.

This kind of contemporary poem has been shaped
and reshaped in particular ways by many poets. And
the finest of these poems brim from the particular, the
regional, the personal, and become—as all successful
poems must—"parables" that say something finally
about our own lives, as well as the lives of their authors.
Additionally, though so much in these poems is in-
formal, the poems "work"; they slip from the instance
and become the exemplum of the general; they glow
with unmistakable universal meaning. Design, tone, pas-
sion—they are doing their good work here, too.

"Negative Capability"

Negative capability is not a contemporary concept, but
a phrase originating with Keats. His idea was, simply
but momentously, that the poet should be a kind of
negative force—that only by remaining himself negative,
or in some way empty, is the poet able to fill himself
with an understanding of, or sympathy for, or empathy

Workday
LINDA HOGAN

I go to work
though there are those who were missing today
from their homes.
I ride the bus
and I do not think of children without food
or how my sisters are chained to prison beds.

I go to the university
and out for lunch
and listen to the higher-ups
tell me all they have read
about Indians
and how to analyze this poem.
They know us
better than we know ourselves.

I ride the bus home
and sit behind the driver.
We talk about the weather
and not enough exercise.
I don't mention Victor Jara's mutilated hands
or men next door
in exile
or my own family's grief over the lost child.

When I get off the bus
I look back at the light in the windows
and the heads bent
and how the women are all alone

in each seat
framed in the windows
and the men are coming home,
then I see them walking on the Avenue,
the beautiful feet,
the perfect legs
even with their spider veins,
the broken knees
with pins in them,
the thighs with their cravings,
the pelvis
and small back
with its soft down,
the shoulders which bend forward
and forward and forward
to protect the heart from pain.

with, the subject of his poem. Here is a passage (from
a letter to his brothers)* in which he discusses it:

> "it struck me, what quality went to form a Man
> of Achievement especially in Literature & which
> Shakespeare possessed so enormously—I mean
> *Negative Capability,* that is when a man is
> capable of being in uncertainties, Mysteries,
> doubts, without any irritable reaching after fact
> & reason— . . ."

And he goes on,

> "Coleridge, for instance, would let go by a fine
> isolated verisimilitude caught from the Pene-
> tralium of mystery, from being incapable of re-
> maining content with half knowledge. This
> pursued through Volumes would perhaps take
> us no further than this, that with a great poet
> the sense of Beauty overcomes every other con-
> sideration, or rather obliterates all considera-
> tion."

Keats elsewhere writes of "taking part" in the life of the
sparrow pecking crumbs at his window. "A Poet is
the most unpoetical of any thing in existence," he
says in still another letter, "because he has no Identi-
ty—he is continually in for—and filling some other

The Letters of John Keats, edited by Hyder Edward Rollins (Cambridge:
Harvard University Press, 1958), Volume 1, p. 193.

Body— . . ."* Neither was Keats bothered by the cat-
egories of animate and inanimate: his friend Richard
Woodhouse records that Keats claimed he could "con-
ceive of a billiard Ball that it may have a sense of delight
from its own roundness, smoothness & very volubility
& the rapidity of its motion."†

Now, as then, the concept of negative capability goes
to the heart of the matter—the "mere" diction of the
poem, in any age, is the vehicle that holds, then transfers
from the page to the reader an absolutely essential qual-
ity of real feeling. Poetry cannot happen without it; and
no one has talked about it more usefully and marvelously
than Keats; his commentary is as up-to-date as a sunrise.

Poems by Type

The Lyric Poem

The poem most popular today is the fairly brief lyric
poem. By fairly brief I mean to sixty lines or so, and
probably shorter. A glance into any current anthology
will quickly show how many poems of this type and
length are being written, compared with poems of great
length, or extreme brevity.

This lyric poem is brief, concentrated, has usually
no more than a single subject and focus and no more
than a single voice, and is more likely to employ a simple
and natural rather than an intricate or composed mu-

---

*Ibid. Letter to Richard Woodhouse, October 27, 1818.
†Ibid. Letter from Richard Woodhouse to John Taylor, about October
27, 1818.

sicality. It is not unlike a simple coiled spring, waiting to release its energy in a few clear phrases.

The Narrative Poem

The narrative poem is generally longer than the lyric poem, and its tone is without such a tightly coiled force. It is discursive, it pauses for moments of humor and slowly unfolding description. It sets an easy and readable pace, and helps us to enjoy sequential events. At times, in the lyric poem, we feel we are in a vortex; when we listen to the narrative poem, we are comfortable. Engaged, and at times entranced, we could listen for hours. We do not love anything more deeply than we love a story—narrative is at the center of all literature.

Whittier's *Snowbound* is a narrative poem. So is Keats's *The Eve of St. Agnes,* Walter de la Mare's *The Listener,* and Robert Penn Warren's *The Ballad of Billie Potts.*

The Longer Poem

No one writes epic poems now. But poets do write long poems, ambitious poems, with a central idea, digressions, and often different voices. Generally speaking, such poems contain many kinds of writing, according to the subject of the passage and the author's inclination. Such poems include many of the great works of our century: Williams's *Paterson,* MacLeish's *Conquistador,* R. P. Warren's *Audubon: A Vision,* Hart Crane's *The Bridge,* T. S. Eliot's *The Waste Land,* for example.

Very long poems are not necessarily epic poems.

The epic poem requires a dignified theme, organic unity, and an orderly progress of the action,* with a heroic figure or figures. *Beowulf* is an epic poem; so are the *Iliad* and the *Odyssey*.

The Prose Poem

The prose poem is too recent a form to have developed a tradition, and so definitions are hard to come by. What you see on the page is a fairly short block of type—a paragraph or two, rarely more than a page. It looks like prose. Perhaps it has characters, perhaps not. Often, it is pure description. It usually does have the same sense of difference from worldly or sequential time that one feels in a poem. And it does certainly ask to be read with the same concentration, and allowance for the fanciful and the experimental, that we give to the poem.

Because the prose poem is brief—or perhaps just because it is something other than a poem—it seems more often than not to have at its center a situation rather than a narrative. Nothing much *happens,* that is, except this: through particularly fresh and intense writing, something happens to the reader—one's felt response to the "situation" of the prose poem grows fresh and intense also.

What is especially fascinating about prose poems is the problem of making the language work *without the musicality of the line.* The syntax found in prose poems is often particularly exquisite, combining power and

---

*So said Aristotle.

grace. In fact, the prose of prose poems is often a real advertisement for the simple power and endless nuance of the English language.

Writers interested in this form should turn first to the prose poems of Charles Baudelaire and Arthur Rimbaud. James Wright and Robert Bly both published prose poems during the seventies, and even earlier. The number of poets who now at least occasionally write and publish prose poems is large, and growing larger.

Inappropriate Language

Because every poem is a new creation and because the creative force often makes sweet use of the most unlikely apparatus, it is not always possible, or wise, to set down absolutely firm rules. Yet this can certainly be said: in almost any poem certain practices are appropriate, certain practices are inappropriate.

Poetic Diction

Poetic diction is language in which all freshness is gone, from which credibility has long vanished, in which "the edge is off." The actual forming of the world of the poem, in the imagination, can't happen when poetic diction is used because the words or images are, simply, out of electricity. They are no longer functional words or images—instead they merely serve as points of reference to tell us what kind of thing is meant. They are stand-ins for a real thing that is not there. When we hear them we don't respond: we only go through the old gestures of an accustomed response. And nothing kills a poem more quickly—for the poem, if it works at all, works as a statement that is experienced by the imagination, eliciting real rather than conditioned responses.

The language of poetic diction is romantic and its images come from the natural world. Patches of woods are "bowers"; fields are "emerald carpets"; trees are Druids or statesmen perhaps; the moonlight is a river; birds are members of a choir; the sun is the eye of heaven; and the sea is a briny bed. And so forth. It is a collection of real clunkers. It is language that is stale, mirthful when it does not mean to be, and empty. Avoid it.

The Cliché

The cliché works in poems as it works in any kind of writing—badly. Do not use the cliché in a poem unless, perhaps, you are writing a poem about the cliché.

Inversion

Inversion—changing the normal word order—is usually thought of as a bad thing. Of course it isn't, necessarily. When it is a useful change, we admire it. When it doesn't work, it stands out imprudently, it feels "out of whack," contorted, and we want things put back into their usual order—subject/predicate, subject/predicate.

Bad inversion occurs primarily in metrical verse, and especially in rhymed metrical verse, where it becomes instantly apparent why the sentence has been shifted about—so that the poet could employ the only rhyme he could think of.

But inversion takes place in free verse too. And always, just as when one exchanges an iambic foot for a trochaic foot, the inverted line calls attention to itself.

If you do not want a particular line to be especially noticed, if you are not striving for a specific emphasis when you manipulate the sentence, it is a good idea to question why you are doing what you are doing, and whether you should. Good inversion is wonderful. Good inversion is difficult to achieve. Bad inversion is never wonderful and rarely difficult to achieve.

Informational Language

There is a kind of language that is clearly unsuitable when one is writing a poem. I call it informational language. It is the language one would use if one were writing a paragraph on how to operate a can opener. It is a language that means to be crisp and accurate. Its words are exact. They do not ever desire to throw two shadows. The language is cold. It does not reach for any territory beyond the functional.

Appropriate Language

Syntax

Proper syntax never hurt anyone. Correct grammar and forceful, graceful syntax give the poem a vigor that it has to have. Just as the ellipsis, which is trying to imply a weighty "something" that has not been said but that

the poet wants felt, is a construct of weakness, so too
is the dangling phrase. The phrase with no verb—no
action and no placement—is more apt to sink the ship
than to float it.

Every adjective and adverb is worth five cents. Every
verb is worth fifty cents.

Variety Versus Habits

Effective writing varies its ingredients.

I once was given a poem in which all nouns, verbs,
and even adjectives were doubled. Every one of them.
This kind of writing points to one thing only—a bad
habit that has not yet been discovered. One of the real
values of the workshop is the possibility that someone
will notice one's lackluster, monotonous, and persistent
habits, and point them out. If you do not think this is
one of the most important things you can do for yourself,
or beg someone to do for you, think again.

The Simple or the Complicated

From time to time I have heard students complain that
the advice of their elders is always the same—that they
should write simply, freshly, and clearly—while at the
same time many of the poems used as models are highly
organized, complicated, and difficult. It is true. The
reasoning is as follows: (1) The beginning writer should
learn to construct the poem simply, freshly, and clearly,
and then (2) the beginning writer will no longer be a
beginning writer and can go on to more complicated,
highly organized, and difficult work.

A Note of Caution

Finally, let me return to the important caution with which I ended a previous chapter: language is a vibrant, malleable, living material. In the writing of the poem, nothing, if it is done well and works to the desired effect, is wrong. This is true concerning all matters of technique, and it is true also concerning diction and tone and voice. We have momentous examples from poems themselves, and the good guidance of fine writers, and our own common good sense. We can know a lot. And still, no doubt, there are rash and wonderful ideas brewing somewhere; there are many surprises yet to come.

Imagery

THE LANGUAGE OF THE POEM is the language of particulars. Without it, poetry might still be wise, but it would surely be pallid. And thin. It is the detailed, sensory language incorporating images that gives the poem dash and tenderness. And authenticity. Poems are "imaginary gardens with real toads in them," said Marianne Moore.

How is it done? What is meant by "particulars?" What are images? How does this figurative language work?

Imagery means, generally, the representation of one thing by another thing. A statue is an image. When Robert Burns wrote, "O, my luve is like a red red rose," that rose is an image; Burns was using imagery. If Burns had written "My love is sweet, wild, wonderful, you would like her," he would have been using descriptive language, but no imagery. There is, in the second sentence, no representative image of the beloved person.

Figurative language is another term for imagery. When we talk about figurative language, we mean that in the poem there is a figure—an image—that is, a concrete, nonliteral, informing representation of something. This "something" might be a person, a thing, or an abstraction. One could represent patience, for example, as a figure on a monument—a quality as patient as stone, in other words.

Usually the term is used when one of the specific devices of figurative language is meant—for example, a metaphor or simile, allusion or personification.* When we talk about "a figure of speech," we are talking about an instance of figurative language.

Such figures may be straightforward, like the red rose in Burns's poem. Or they may be as complicated as the figure in the concluding lines of William Butler Yeats's poem *The Second Coming:*

> And what *rough beast,*† its hour come round at last,
> Slouches towards Bethlehem to be born?

In addition, the poem must have a necessary quality of detail—enough to sustain the reader's passage into the imagined world of the poem. I call it the poem's texture. This is where the "particulars" come in.

---

*These terms are defined in later sections of the chapter.
†Italics mine.

The Particulars and the Texture of the Poem

When you use the words "the apple" or "the peach" you are representing a *thing*. Neither is a very specific thing, yet both are visual things compared, for example, to the word "fruit," which is informational only and which the reader will understand, but from which no particular image can form.

If you drop the article and use the word alone—"apple" or "peach"—you are moving away from the direction of the particular and toward the abstract. Once again, the reader can visualize "the apple" or "an apple," but "apple" is only a word meaning any or all apples—it is not a thing. Thus it is unseeable, it vanishes from the realm of the imagined real. The world is full of sensory detail. The poem needs this sensory detail also.

When one writes "the last apple on the tree," or "the one small peach as pink as dawn," one is beginning to deal with particulars—to develop texture.

This is a good moment to read Elizabeth Bishop's poem *The Fish*. There are metaphors and similes in the poem, devices discussed later. Also there is texture—the poet gives the reader a plentitude of details concerning the fish, and this texture is vital to the poem. Such texture is vital to all poetry. It is what makes the poem an experience, something much more than mere statement.

The Fish

ELIZABETH BISHOP

I caught a tremendous fish
and held him beside the boat
half out of water, with my hook
fast in a corner of his mouth.
He didn't fight.
He hadn't fought at all.
He hung a grunting weight,
battered and venerable
and homely. Here and there
his brown skin hung in strips
like ancient wallpaper,
and its pattern of darker brown
was like wallpaper:
shapes like full-blown roses
stained and lost through age.
He was speckled with barnacles,
fine rosettes of lime,
and infested
with tiny white sea-lice,
and underneath two or three
rags of green weed hung down.
While his gills were breathing in
the terrible oxygen
—the frightening gills,
fresh and crisp with blood,
that can cut so badly—
I thought of the coarse white flesh
packed in like feathers,

the big bones and the little bones,
the dramatic reds and blacks
of his shiny entrails,
and the pink swim-bladder
like a big peony.
I looked into his eyes
which were far larger than mine
but shallower, and yellowed,
the irises backed and packed
with tarnished tinfoil
seen through the lenses
of old scratched isinglass.
They shifted a little, but not
to return my stare.
—It was more like the tipping
of an object toward the light.
I admired his sullen face,
the mechanism of his jaw,
and then I saw
that from his lower lip
—if you could call it a lip—
grim, wet, and weaponlike,
hung five old pieces of fish-line,
or four and a wire leader
with the swivel still attached,
with all their five big hooks
grown firmly in his mouth.
A green line, frayed at the end
where he broke it, two heavier lines,
and a fine black thread
still crimped from the strain and snapped
when it broke and he got away.
Like medals with their ribbons

frayed and wavering,
a five-haired beard of wisdom
trailing from his aching jaw.
I stared and stared
and victory filled up
the little rented boat,
from the pool of bilge
where oil had spread a rainbow
around the rusted engine
to the bailer rusted orange,
the sun-cracked thwarts,
the oarlocks on their strings,
the gunnels—until everything
was rainbow, rainbow, rainbow!
And I let the fish go.

Couldn't Keats have noted the nightingale's song, and his thoughts about it, in a poem far briefer than his *Ode to a Nightingale?* But we would not have been given the texture of the poem—the atmosphere, the very particular details, in which we feel invited to sit with Keats in the garden and feel the song spindling over the fields, its deliciousness and melancholy, and all the questions thereby evoked.

I can think of no part of the poem that is more essential than this matter of its texture. How much of it is needed depends on many factors, of course, on the pace of the poem, and on how good you are. Whitman, in a single line, can establish the reader thoroughly in the place-where-the-poem-is:

Over the sharp-peak'd farm house, with its scallop'd scum and slender shoots from the gutters, . . .

(Song of Myself, section 33)

or:

The shape of the step-ladder for the convicted and sentenced murderer, the murderer with haggard face and pinion'd arms, . . .

(Song of the Broad Axe, section 10)

No, it does not take much, but it takes a sure eye and a capable hand to be forever noticing and writing down

such particulars. When reading Stanley Kunitz's poem
The Round, I think of the poet leaning closer and closer
into the flowers, so that he sees not just how the light
flowed over the honeybees, but how

> down blue-spiked veronica
> light flowed in rivulets
> over the humps of the honeybees; . . .

The poet must not only write the poem but must scru-
tinize the world intensely, or anyway that part of the
world he or she has taken for subject. If the poem is
thin, it is likely so not because the poet does not know
enough words, but because he or she has not stood long
enough among the flowers—has not seen them in any
fresh, exciting, and valid way.

Figurative Language

The language of the poem is also the language of one
thing compared to another thing.

   In figurative language, a familiar thing is linked to
an unknown thing, as a key, to unlock the mystery, or
some part of the mystery, of the thing that is unknown.

   In every instance *something has to be known initially*
in order for the linkage and the informing quality of the
comparison to work.

   An image is frequently a pictorial phrase, which
delineates or captures some essence of a known thing.
In the metaphoric device, this essence is then extended
so that it applies to an unknown thing. The chosen

The Round
STANLEY KUNITZ

Light splashed this morning
on the shell-pink anemones
swaying on their tall stems;
down blue-spiked veronica
light flowed in rivulets
over the humps of the honeybees;
this morning I saw light kiss
the silk of the roses
in their second flowering,
my late bloomers
flushed with their brandy.
A curious gladness shook me.

So I have shut the doors of my house,
so I have trudged downstairs to my cell,
so I am sitting in semi-dark
hunched over my desk
with nothing for a view
to tempt me
but a bloated compost heap,
steamy old stinkpile,
under my window;
and I pick my notebook up
and I start to read aloud
the still-wet words I scribbled
on the blotted page:
"Light splashed . . ."

I can scarcely wait till tomorrow
when a new life begins for me,
as it does each day,
as it does each day.

phrase is believed to be suitable—that is, we have a faith that the poet will have chosen something suitable—both to the known and to the unknown thing. This transfer of some quality of the known to the unknown is like a beam of light; we "see" (that is, we understand) something about the unknown in the light of the known.

> Love like a burning city in the breast.
> (Edna St. Vincent Millay, *Fatal Interview,* XXVI)

> O to break loose, like the chinook
> salmon jumping and falling back, . . .
> (Robert Lowell, *Waking Early Sunday Morning*)

Additionally, such an image can be used to link one known thing to another known thing in order to help us "see" (physically see) something more sharply and memorably:

> The clouds were low and hairy in the skies,
> Like locks blown forward in the gleam of eyes.
> (Robert Frost, *Once by the Pacific*)

Simile

The *simile* uses the words "like" or "as" in its construction. Thus the three illustrations just given are all similes. One thing is "like" another thing, or one thing does something "as" another thing does it. The simile is an explicit, stated comparison.

. . . the child's cry opens like a knife-blade.
>   (Donald Hall, *Twelve Seasons*)

I wandered lonely as a cloud
>   (William Wordsworth, *I Wandered Lonely* . . .)

When the minted gold in the vault smiles like the
        night-watchman's daughter, . . .
>   (Walt Whitman, *A Song for Occupations,* #6)

Metaphor

The *metaphor* is an implicit rather than an explicit com-
parison. It does not use the words "like" or "as" in its
construction. The two things compared often seem very
different, and the linkage often surprises and delights
as well as it enlightens. Donald Hall says "The new
metaphor is a miracle, like the creation of life."*

Little boys lie still, awake,
Wondering, wondering,
Delicate little boxes of dust.
>   (James Wright, *The Undermining
>   of the Defense Economy*)

And she balanced in the delight of her thought,
A wren, happy, tail into the wind,

The Pleasures of Poetry (New York: Harper & Row, 1971), p. 23.

Her song trembling the twigs and small branches.
(Theodore Roethke, Elegy for Jane)

When a comparison of two things generally is repeated and extended throughout a poem, with repeated instances of imagery, it is called an *extended metaphor.* When the comparison is particularly unusual or fanciful, it may be called a *conceit.*

Personification

Personification is the term used when one gives a physical characteristic or innate quality of animation to something that is inanimate, or to an abstraction. James Wright's lines—"I bowed my head, and heard the sea far off / Washing its hands"—contain a personification.* The last two lines of the Emily Dickinson stanza quoted earlier, on page 41—"It was not Night, for all the Bells / Put out their Tongues, for Noon"—is another example.

Here is still another:

The yellow fog that rubs its back upon the
   window-panes,
The yellow smoke that rubs its muzzle on the
   window-panes,
Licked its tongue into the corners of the
   evening,
Lingered upon the pools that stand in drains,

---

*From *At the Slackening of the Tide.*

Let fall upon its back the soot that falls from
   chimneys,
Slipped by the terrace, made a sudden leap,
And seeing that it was a soft October night,
Curled once about the house, and fell asleep.

                  (T. S. Eliot, *The Love Song
                  of J. Alfred Prufrock*)

Personification is an enlivening and joyful device. The
challenge, of course, is to do it well. What you say about
the abstraction or inanimate object must make sense of
some sort—note how all the movements of the fog are
horizontal, and how the pace of the movements keeps
changing—all quite foglike. Though each movement is
precise, and impossible, it is, in some wild magical way,
possible to imagine it. And, a delight to imagine it.
Simply to have trees wave, or waves dance, will not do.
Better no personification than bad or foolish personifi-
cation.

Allusion

An *allusion* is a reference to something that belongs
properly to a world beyond the specific sphere of the
poem. Often the reference comes from an historical or
a cultural context, but not necessarily. Its use is to
deepen the definition of or to extend the quality of
something in the poem. Example: referring to William
Blake's poem *The Sunflower* or to van Gogh's paintings
of sunflowers would deepen and extend a perception
of "any" sunflower growing in a field. Through the al-

lusion, the values of literature and art are linked to the casual flower; through the allusion they shed their own intrinsic and valuable light upon it.

Universal Images

We experience the physical world around us through our five senses. Through our imagination and our intelligence, we recall, organize, conceptualize, and meditate. What we meditate upon is never shapeless or filled with alien emotion—it is filled with all the precise earthly things that we have ever encountered and all of our responses to them. The task of the meditation is to put disorder into order. No one could think, without first living among things. No one would need to think, without the initial profusion of perceptual experience.

Since we live in one world, and each of us is given the same five senses, and each of us has evolved on the same road out of the forest and the jungle, we all share a universal fund of perceptions. This common fund includes personal experiences and events that are likely to occur within the span of each lifetime; they touch upon community life, social life, spiritual life. Within this fund are perceptions so ancient, dramatic, and constant that they have been, over the centuries, mythologized. They have been inexorably bound up in each of us with certain reliable responses.

I am speaking of such archetypal concepts as the ocean as mother, the sun as a symbol of health and hope, the return of spring as resurrection, the bird as a symbol of the spirit, the lion as an emblem of courage, the rose as an example of ephemeral beauty—concepts that link some object or action of the natural world on the one hand, and our all but preordained response to it on the other.

These days many poets live in cities, or at least in suburbs, and the natural world grows ever more distant from our everyday lives. Most people, in fact, live in cities, and therefore most readers are not necessarily very familiar with the natural world. And yet the natural world has always been the great warehouse of symbolic imagery. Poetry is one of the ancient arts, and it began, as did all the fine arts, within the original wilderness of the earth. Also, it began through the process of seeing, and feeling, and hearing, and smelling, and touching, and then remembering—I mean *remembering in words*—what these perceptual experiences were like, while trying to describe the endless invisible fears and desires of our inner lives. The poet used the actual, known event or experience to elucidate the inner, invisible experience—or, in other words, the poet used figurative language, relying for those figures on the natural world.

Certainly imagery can be gleaned from the industrial world—what do Blake's "dark Satanic Mills,"* for example, owe to the natural world? The city can be, and has been, the source of firm poetic description, and imagery too. But the natural world is the old river that runs through everything, and I think poets will forever fish along its shores.

Additionally, it is obvious that the literature of our

---

*From *And Did Those Feet.*

world cannot be read—*felt* as well as understood—
without a familiarity with the natural world. The reader
without perceptual experience with the natural pro-
cesses is locked out of the poetry of our world. What
would Yeats's "rough beast" mean to such a reader?
Or the "red red rose" of Burns? Indeed, what would
Romeo's amazed outcry

"It is the east, and Juliet is the sun!—"

mean to a reader who is without an intimate feeling for
the way, every morning, the light rises and blazes against
the darkness?

Literature is not just words, neither is it just ideas.
It is a formal construct mirroring all of life, reporting
it, questioning it. And the power of poetry comes from
both mental inquiry and figurative language—the very
mud and leaves of the world. Without this mud and
leaves—and fish and roses and honeybees—the poem
would be as dull as a mumble. Without figurative lan-
guage we could have no literature. A *body* of literature,
as it is called.

Some Cautions

There are no rules about using imagery. Certainly it
enlivens and deepens the poem. It is a source of delight.
It makes the poem more meaningful—more of an ex-
perience. It is powerful stuff.

How much one uses it is a matter of taste. The writer
would be wise to remember, however, just how much
emotional excitement it can create. The poem that, all

along its line of endeavor, pauses to give out "jolts" of imagery may end up like a carnival ride: the reader has been lurched, and has laughed—has been all but whiplashed—but has gotten nowhere. In the shed electricity of too much imagery the purpose of the ride— and a sense of arrival—may be lost.

There is also the question of imagery that is fit and imagery that may be unfit. This too is a matter of taste. Poetry is a serious business; literature is the apparatus through which the world tries to keep intact its important ideas and feelings. It is joyful, and funny too sometimes, but it is neither facile nor poisonous. If you are not sure your image is appropriate, don't use it. Imagery that is inappropriate, or excessive, or self-indulgent, is offensive.

Figurative language can give shape to the difficult and the painful. It can make visible and "felt" that which is invisible and "unfeelable." Imagery, more than anything else, can take us out of our own existence and let us stand in the condition of another instance, or another life. It can make the subject of the poem, whatever it is, as intimate as honey—or ashes—in the mouth. Use it responsibly.

Revision

WHAT YOU ARE FIRST able to write on the page, whether the writing comes easily or with difficulty, is not likely to be close to a finished poem. If it has arrived without much effort, so much the better; if it was written with great toil, that does not matter either. What matters is that you consider what you have on the page as an unfinished piece of work that now requires your best conscious and patient appraisal.

One of the difficult tasks of rewriting is to separate yourself sufficiently from the origins of the poem—your own personal connections to it. Without this separation, it is hard for the writer to judge whether the written piece has all the information it needs—the details, after all, are so vivid in your own mind. On the other hand, because of this very sense of ownership, the poem is often burdened with a variety of "true" but unhelpful details.

Poems begin in experience, but poems are not in

fact experience, nor even a necessarily exact reportage of an experience. They are imaginative constructs, and they do not exist to tell us about the poet or the poet's actual experience—they exist in order to be poems. John Cheever says somewhere in his journals, "I lie, in order to tell a more significant truth." The poem, too, is after "a more significant truth." Loyalty to the actual experience—whatever got the poem started—is not necessarily helpful; often it is a hindrance.

I like to say that I write poems for a stranger who will be born in some distant country hundreds of years from now. This is a useful notion, especially during revision. It reminds me, forcefully, that everything necessary must be on the page. I must make a complete poem—a river-swimming poem, a mountain-climbing poem. Not *my* poem, if it's well done, but a deeply breathing, bounding, self-sufficient poem. Like a traveler in an uncertain land, it needs to carry with it all that it must have to sustain its own life—and not a lot of extra weight, either.

A caution: there are poems that are packed full of interesting and beautiful lines—metaphors on top of metaphors—details depending from details. Such poems slide this way and that way, they never say something but they say it twice, or thrice. Clearly they are very clever poems. Forsaken however in such writing is the pace—the *energy* between the start and the finish, the sense of flow, movement, and integrity. Finally the great weight of its glittering pulls it down. How much wiser to keep a little of the metaphoric glitter in one's pocket, and let the poem maintain, without excessive interruption, its forward flow. *Cutting* is an important part of revision.

In truth, revision is an almost endless task. But it is endlessly fascinating, too, and especially in the early years it is a process in which much is learned.

In my own work, I usually revise through forty or fifty drafts of a poem before I begin to feel content with it. Other poets take longer. Have some lines come to you, a few times, nearly perfect, as easily as a dream arranges itself during sleep? That's luck. That's grace. But *this* is the usual way: hard work, hard work, hard work. *This* is the way it is done.

It is good to remember how many sweet and fine poems there are in the world—I mean, it is a help to remember that out of writing, and the rewriting, beauty is born.

It is good also to remember that, now and again, it is simply best to throw a poem away. Some things are unfixable.

Workshops
and Solitude

Instruction, Discussion, Advice

A WORKSHOP can help writers in a number of important ways. Let us look at some of the possibilities.

First, a workshop can, in an organized way, make sure that members of the group learn the necessary language of their craft. Without this language, useful discussion is difficult and slow—members of the workshop cannot talk about poems with any ease and specificity. Neither can they read and understand books or articles relating to prosody, which, if they continue in the creative writing field, they need to be able to do.

Second, with the use of this common language, members of a workshop can save each other enormous amounts of time. I mean, years! They meet to support one another's efforts, and to encourage one another, but not to encourage bad writing. The general goal of better writing gives each person the obligation to point out, in the poems offered for discussion, what they think works effectively, and what they think does not.

There will be differences of opinion, of course. The point of the workshop is not to settle such disputes, but to look into each instance as closely and neutrally as possible—that is, to discuss the poems, or passages from poems, in terms of technique rather than taste—to suggest *why* something works or does not work, whether or not one finds it thumpingly lovely, or perfectly awful.

The primary subject of the workshop is not aesthetics, after all, but the writing skills of its members.

With everyone using an understandable language, and with a number of persons scrutinizing the work, the workshop members can learn a great deal about their general aptitude and specific writing skills—can learn much more than even the most diligent writer could ascertain in the same amount of time while working alone.

And, of course, such knowledge about one's work is essential before improvement or even change can begin.

These are two completely useful and wonderful things that a workshop can do.

As I indicated at the beginning of this book, I see no reason why beginning writers cannot profit from imitative writing, or assignments in which the writers are meant to explore a specific technique consciously and deliberately to get the feel of it, as it were, without, for the moment, the weighty responsibility of writing a genuine poem. In every class I have ever taught, two or three weeks of such exercises have been of real benefit. Such writing is often poor and awkward stuff, but that is to be expected, since it is writing-on-demand. A little creative mess on paper does no harm, however. The point is that students can begin, with such exercises, to move out of their already rigid habits. They can learn that they don't have to write as they have been writing—that there are other ways—that there are *innumerable* ways.

It is fun, also, as well as profitable—and not necessarily easy either—to imitate the work of known poets, to write a "Whitman poem," using his kind of long line, or a quick-stepping, deftly unfolding "Williams poem," that is, to work consciously with sound, line, imagery, and diction. Through such exercises, a workshop begins to give the writers choices. The workshop cannot give the writer expertise—that, he or she may come to later, after long and solitary work. But the understanding of technique, which is the door to choice—this will send the student along the right path toward singularity, authority, and power.

Luck, diligence, spontaneity, and inspiration are all needed to write a poem. Of course! Which only makes the case for long and deep study of technique stronger, I think, for if the task needs all of these, surely every bit of technical skill a person can bring to it is to his or her advantage. The poem is an attitude, and a prayer; it sings on the page and it sings itself off the page; it lives through genius *and* technique.

The risk of the workshop is that it is necessarily composed of a group of persons and it therefore cannot avoid certain patterns of social behavior. It is natural for people in a group to try to get along with each other. It is natural for each person in a group to want to be liked by the others. One's writing is a kind of mirror of one's self. One hopes that one's poems will be liked, if not loudly and consistently praised. And this, if we are not careful, can determine the kind of poems that are written, or, anyway, are brought into the group for discussion.

A writer may give up some rough but unusual fashioning of lines that either can't find favor with the group, or is so imperfectly done that it elicits criticism for its raw execution, though the idea behind it be something well worth cherishing. What a shame! I would rather see an ambitious though rough poem than a careful and tame poem. I would rather see writers study their problems, living with them as best they can, than to "solve" by deletion or by toning the poem down to something easier to accomplish. Deletion teaches nothing. It is a responsibility of the instructor, I think, to see that students do not "bank their fires" in order to gain a little passing praise.

Nor is this all that is difficult in the workshop. Sometimes, out of this wish to be liked (but we think of it as a wish to be kind), criticism is disarmed. One wants to praise, or one wants to be silent. But the workshop does not operate on silence. Again, I find that a common language is of the greatest help here. By keeping the emphasis on technical matters, on language constructs, discussion can go on, and be neither too sharp, nor too dull, nor too personal. It is never much use to say that a poem works, or fails, without saying why. Discussion must go beyond opinion and beyond personal taste, if it is to put options in the students' hands. This is another of the instructor's responsibilities—to set the mood of a criticism in which enthusiasm, not disappointment, is the tone. But all voices in the workshop can help, by knowing the language, and by a generally good-spirited attitude, which is patient, absorbed, and endlessly loyal to each writer's intention.

The best thing about workshops is that people learn there that they can change, they can write better and differently from what they had always thought themselves capable of, and this is so often the good news they have been waiting for that all the perils are small beside it. It is a great pleasure to see people surpass what they thought was the measure of their ability.

It is also the pleasure of the workshop that everyone there gets to be a part of such moments of sweetness, when there appears at last a poem that is fine and shapely, where before there was only struggle, and the tangled knots of words. We all partake, then, a little, of the miracle, that is made not only of luck and inspiration and even happenstance, but of those other matters too—technical knowledge and diligent work—matters that are less interesting perhaps, but altogether essential, for such things support the ineffable and moving light of the poem: they are the bedrock of the river.

Solitude

It is no use thinking, however, that the writing of poems—the actual writing—can accommodate itself to a social setting, even to the most sympathetic social setting of a workshop composed of loyal friends. It cannot. The work improves there and often the will to work gets valuable nourishment and ideas. But, for good reason, the poem requires of the writer not society or instruction, but a patch of profound and unbroken solitude.

This is the reason. The poem, as it starts to form in the writer's mind, and on paper, can't abide interruption. I don't mean that it *won't* but that it *can't*. When writing, as nearly as is imaginatively possible (and that is very near indeed), one is undertaking the action, or has become the character (think of what Keats said), in the unfolding scene or action of the poem. To interrupt the writer from the line of thought is to wake the dreamer from the dream. The dreamer cannot enter that dream, precisely as it was unfolding, ever again because the line of thought is more than that: it is a line of feeling as well. Until interruption occurs, this feeling is as real as the desk on which the poet is working. For the poem is not nailed together, or formed from one logical point to another, which might be retrievable—it is created, through work in which the interweavings of craft, thought, and feeling are intricate, mysterious, and altogether "mortal." Interrupt—and the whole structure can collapse. An interruption into the writing of a poem is as severe as any break into a passionate run of feeling. The story of Coleridge dreaming his way through *Kubla Khan* until the visitor from Porlock rapped upon his door is equally understandable whether Coleridge was actually asleep dreaming a dream, or dreaming-working. The effect is the same.

It is appropriate and useful to begin writing poems in a group, a class, or a workshop. Then, as one becomes more skilled, there is a natural and necessary movement away from the group. The writer now wants less discussion, fewer commentators. The writer now has a much clearer idea of what he or she wants to do—there is not so much need for ideas as there is for application, and for self-communing. There will always remain intervals of pleasure and illumination among friends and other poets. But, finally, one realizes that one *may* be ready for the real work. On that day the writer understands that solitude is the necessity, and leaves friends, and workshops, and handbooks, and heads for it, diligently and resolutely.

Conclusion

NO ONE CAN TELL YOU how best to make the writing happen. For one poet at least, short naps have proved helpful; for him, leaving consciousness for a brief time is invitational to the inner, "poetic" voice.* For myself, walking works in a similar way. I walk slowly and not to get anywhere in particular, but because the motion somehow helps the poem to begin. I end up, usually, standing still, writing something down in the small notebook I always have with me.

For yourself, neither napping nor walking has to be the answer. But, something is. The point is to try various activities or arrangements until you find out what works for you.

Especially when writers are just starting out, the emphasis should be not only upon what they write, but

---

*See *Goatfoot Milktongue Twinbird* by Donald Hall (Ann Arbor: The University of Michigan Press, 1978), pp. 3–4.

equally upon the process of writing. A successful class is a class where no one feels that "writer's block" is a high-priority subject.

Said William Blake, "I am not ashamed, afraid, or averse to tell you what Ought to be Told. That I am under the direction of Messengers from Heaven, Daily & Nightly."*

Early in my life I determined not to teach because I like teaching very much. I thought if I was going to be a *real* poet—that is, write the best poetry I possibly could—I would have to guard my time and energy for its production, and thus I should not, as a daily occupation, do anything else that was interesting. Of necessity I worked for many years at many occupations. None of them, in keeping with my promise, was interesting.

Among the things I learned in those years were two of special interest to poets. First, that one can rise early in the morning and have time to write (or, even, to take a walk and then write) before the world's work schedule begins. Also, that one can live simply and honorably on just about enough money to keep a chicken alive. And do so cheerfully.

This I have always known—that if I did not live my life immersed in the one activity which suits me, and which also, to tell the truth, keeps me utterly happy and intrigued, I would come someday to bitter and mortal regret.

---

*From his letter to Thomas Butts, January 10, 1802.

John Cage in a *New York Times* interview* talked about the composer Arnold Schoenberg, with whom he had studied. Said Cage, "He [Schoenberg] gave his students little comfort. When we followed the rules in writing counterpoint, he would say, 'Why don't you take a little liberty?' And when we took liberties, he would say, 'Don't you know the rules?' "

I cherish two sentences and keep them close to my desk. The first is by Flaubert. I came upon it among van Gogh's letters. It says, simply, "Talent is long patience, and originality an effort of will and of intense observation."

Put aside for a moment what Flaubert is *not* talking about—the impulse toward writing, the inspiration and the mystery—and instead look at what he does say: "patience" is necessary, and "an effort of will," and "intense observation." What a hopeful statement! For who needs to be shy of any of these? No one! How patient are you, and what is the steel of your will, and how well do you look and see the things of this world? If your honest answers are shabby, you can change them. What Flaubert is talking about are skills, after all. You can attend to them, *you can do better,* and then even better—until the sweet taste of improvement is in your mouth. When people ask me if I do not take pleasure in poems I have written, I am astonished. What I think of all the time is how to have more patience, and a wilder will—how to see better, and write better.

**New York Times,* Thursday, June 2, 1992, sec. C, p. 13.

The second statement comes from Emerson's journals. In the context, it is written in past tense; changing the verb to present tense it reads: The poem is a confession of faith.

Which is to say, the poem is not an exercise. It is not "wordplay." Whatever skill or beauty it has, it contains something beyond language devices, and has a purpose other than itself. And it is a part of the sensibility of the writer. I don't mean in any "confessional" way, but that it reflects *from* the writer's point of view—his or her perspective—out of all the sum of his or her experience and thought.

Athletes take care of their bodies. Writers must similarly take care of the sensibility that houses the possibility of poems. There is nourishment in books, other art, history, philosophies—in holiness and in mirth. It is in honest hands-on labor also; I don't mean to indicate a preference for the scholarly life. And it is in the green world—among people, and animals, and trees for that matter, if one genuinely cares about trees. A mind that is lively and inquiring, compassionate, curious, angry, full of music, full of feeling, is a mind full of possible poetry. Poetry is a life-cherishing force. And it requires a vision—a *faith,* to use an old-fashioned term. Yes, indeed. For poems are not words, after all, but fires for the cold, ropes let down to the lost, something as necessary as bread in the pockets of the hungry. Yes, indeed.

Permissions
Acknowledgments

BASHŌ   haiku translated by Robert Bly in *News from the Universe,* edited by Robert Bly, published by Sierra Books. Reprinted by permission of Robert Bly.

ELIZABETH BISHOP   "The Fish" from *The Complete Poems 1927–1979* by Elizabeth Bishop. Copyright © 1979, 1983 by Alice Helen Methfessel. Reprinted by permission of Farrar, Straus & Giroux, Inc.

LUCILLE CLIFTON   "i am accused of tending to the past . . . ," copyright © 1991 by Lucille Clifton. Reprinted from *Quilting: Poems 1987–1990* by Lucille Clifton with the permission of BOA Editions, Ltd., 92 Park Ave., Brockport, NY 14420.

EMILY DICKINSON   from poem #510 and poem #341 in *The Complete Poems of* Emily Dickinson, edited by Thomas H. Johnson, published by The Belknap Press of Harvard University.

T. S. ELIOT   from "The Love Song of J. Alfred Prufrock" from *Collected Poems 1909–1962* by T. S. Eliot. Copyright 1936 by

Harcourt Brace Jovanovich; copyright © 1963, 1964 by T. S. Eliot. Reprinted by permission of Harcourt Brace & Company and Faber and Faber Ltd.

ROBERT FROST "Stopping by Woods on a Snowy Evening" and from "Home Burial," "West-Running Brook," and "Once by the Pacific" from *The Poetry of Robert Frost*, edited by Edward Connery Lathem. Copyright 1923, 1928, 1930, 1939, © 1969 by Henry Holt and Company, Inc. Copyright 1951, © 1956, 1958 by Robert Frost. Copyright © 1967 by Lesley Frost Ballantine. Reprinted by permission of Henry Holt and Company, Inc.

DONALD HALL from "Twelve Seasons" in *The Happy Man* by Donald Hall. Copyright 1986 by Donald Hall. Reprinted by permission of Random House, Inc.

LINDA HOGAN "Workday" by Linda Hogan originally appeared in *Savings,* a collection of poetry by Linda Hogan, Coffee House Press, 1988. Copyright © 1988 by Linda Hogan. Reprinted by permission of Coffee House Press.

STANLEY KUNITZ "The Round" by Stanley Kunitz from *Next-to Last Things.* Copyright © 1985 by Stanley Kunitz. Reprinted by permission of Darhansoff & Verrill Literary Agency on behalf of the author.

ROBERT LOWELL from "Waking Early Sunday Morning" in *Near the Ocean* by Robert Lowell. Copyright © 1967 by Robert Lowell. Reprinted by permission of Farrar, Straus & Giroux, Inc. From "Mr. Edwards and the Spider" in *Lord Weary's Castle,* copyright 1946 and renewed 1974 by Robert Lowell. Reprinted by permission of Harcourt Brace & Company.

EDNA ST. VINCENT MILLAY from "Memorial to D.C.: V. Elegy" and from Sonnet XXVI of *Fatal Interview* by Edna St. Vincent Millay. From *Collected Poems,* HarperCollins. Copyright © 1921, 1931, 1948, 1958 by Edna St. Vincent Millay and Norma Millay Ellis. Reprinted by permission of Elizabeth Barnett, literary executor.

Index